THREE APPROACHES TO ABORTION

PETER KREEFT

THREE APPROACHES
TO ABORTION

A Thoughtful and Compassionate
Guide to Today's Most Controversial Issue

IGNATIUS PRESS   SAN FRANCISCO

Cover photograph:
Kathleen Finley & Masterfile
Cover design by Riz Boncan Marsella

CONTENTS

Preface

This book is designed for two groups of people:

1. for pro-life people to give to their pro-choice friends, to explain themselves and their position as fully as possible in a short book; and
2. for pro-choice or undecided people who want to understand the pro-life position from three angles.

The three angles are:

1. the impersonal (the objective, logical arguments);
2. the personal (the subjective motives); and
3. the interpersonal (the combination of the first two that surfaces in dialogue between pro-choice and pro-life people.

Thus the book has three parts:

1. "The Apple Argument against Abortion", an essay arguing logically, in fifteen steps, from the premise that we know what an apple is to the conclusion that abortion must be outlawed;
2. "Why We Fight: A Pro-Life Motivational Map", a confession of fifteen motives that fuel pro-life work; and
3. "What Happens When an Irresistible Force Meets an Immovable Object? A Typical Pro-Life/Pro-Choice Dialogue", which addresses the fifteen most common pro-choice arguments.

Introduction

Abortion is the single most divisive public issue of our time, as slavery was for the nineteenth century, or as prohibition was for the 1920s. Intelligent, committed pro-lifers will not be satisfied in principle with anything less than the legal prohibition, or abolition, of all abortion (though most pro-lifers are pragmatic enough to accept partial abolitions as incremental steps toward that goal). And intelligent, committed pro-choicers understand this and resist, also in principle, any of these incremental steps. Pro-lifers find it intolerable that the most innocent and vulnerable members of our society and our species are legally slaughtered. Pro-choicers find it intolerable that women be forced by law to bear unwanted children against their will. Neither side can or will budge, in principle.

There are only four things that can possibly be done in such a situation.

First, we could simply accept the current standoff and hope it will not erupt into violence and civil war, as abolitionism did in the nineteenth century. Perhaps if we do nothing the problem will just go away. Obviously this is naïve and irresponsible. It is also unhistorical. Already in the U.S. and Canada some have appeared who have murdered abortionists or even their office workers. They have already done what John Brown did at Harper's Ferry just before the Civil War: to protest violence, they have used violence. There is no reason to think that their ilk will simply disappear, or even diminish.

Second, we could accept the current standoff and put social protections around the dispute to keep it from erupting into war. What these protections are, is not clear. No society has yet solved the problem of assassination by fanatics, especially if the fanatics are willing to die along with their victim for the sake of their cause. The closest any society has come to preventing assassinations is totalitarian dictatorship. There were almost no private assassinations under Stalin, Hitler, Mao, Castro, or Pol Pot; all assassinations were carried out by the government. Hardly a "solution"!

Third, we could hope that one of the two sides will simply go away, or weaken, or give up, or at least quiet down—not out of conviction but simply because of attrition: time, not logic, will solve the problem. I fear this is also wishful thinking, living in denial, and failing to understand the depth of conviction of both sides.

Fourth, we could hope that reason rather than force will convince one side it is wrong. This sounds to many people even more idealistic and unrealistic than the first three options; but it has happened before. Many practices—including both slavery and prohibition, as well as torture, cannibalism, blood vengeance by families, polygamy, and infanticide—have disappeared because humanity became convinced that these were wrong.

It is my hope that this book will help to make a little progress in this direction, the direction of peace not through force but through enlightenment—that is, through truth. Any other peace is perilous, for a peace not based on truth is not true peace. Certainly, any peace based on ignoring truth, scorning truth, indifference to truth, or disbelief in truth cannot be true peace.

I

The Apple Argument
against Abortion

An essay arguing logically in fifteen steps from the premise that we know what an apple is to the conclusion that abortion must be outlawed

One of the stark differences between the "pro-choice" and "pro-life" positions is that the issue of abortion is almost *always* described by the pro-choice people as a "difficult" and "complex" issue, while those words are almost *never* used by the pro-life side. I shall try to prove here not only that it was wrong to legalize abortion, but that it was *clearly* wrong; not only that it was criminal to decriminalize abortion, but that Mother Teresa was exactly on target (as usual) when she said, "If abortion isn't wrong, then nothing is wrong."

The pro-choice media routinely characterize pro-lifers, and their position, as unenlightened, unscientific, and irrational, dependent on rhetoric and religion (which they often confuse), on blind faith or feeling (which they also often confuse), on fear, fallacy, fantasy, or fanaticism. So please consider very carefully how often during this chapter I appeal to feeling and rhetoric *instead of* reason and argument. I may elicit strong feelings from you; I may even make you angry; but I will always give logical reasons for doing so.

My argument is addressed both to pro-choicers, as an attempt at logical persuasion, and to my fellow pro-lifers, as an attempt to clarify logically what many of us know only instinctively. The argument is addressed to everyone because its only premise is one that is known by everyone. The premise is that we all know what an apple is.

The essential strategy of any argument is as follows. A tries to convince B by an argument. So A begins with premises that B also admits, and then tries to show B that these premises logically and necessarily lead to a conclusion that A believes but B does not. Thus, B has only three options: assuming the terms are clear and unambiguous, he must either (1) justify his disagreement with A's conclusion because he denies one of the premises in A's argument; or (2) justify his disagreement with A's conclusion because he has found a logical fallacy in A's argument, so that even though the premises are true the conclusion does not necessarily follow; or, if he cannot do either of these two things, he must (3) change his mind and accept A's conclusion. For if the premises are true and the argument is logically valid, the conclusion must be true.

So I shall argue from non-controversial premise that most pro-choicers also accept: that we know what an apple is. And I shall argue that this premise logically entails the controversial conclusion that abortion must not be legalized. There are fifteen steps to the argument. It is like a fifteen-step ladder. Pro-choicers who want to avoid the conclusion must find some step in the argument, some rung on the ladder, at which to get off. I do not know what step that will be, but I think it will have to be the first one.

1. We know what an apple is

The choice of premises is the choice of an "Archimedean point". (Archimedes said, "Give me a lever and a fulcrum to rest it on and I can move the world.") Imagine two cars at an intersection in Los Angeles. Both roads go straight. One goes due east, the other goes just a few degrees north of east. After the two cars have gone down the two roads for just one mile, they are still close enough to see each other; but by the time they are three thousand miles down the roads, one is in Georgia while the other is in Washington, D. C.

I choose a simple and undeniable first premise because in actual human conversation most arguments move backwards to their premises rather than forward to their conclusions, even though logically all arguments go the other way, from premises to conclusion. When I say we usually move backwards to premises I mean that most disputes are not about corollaries but about assumptions; not about whether to *apply* a principle in this way or that way, but about how to *justify* a principle. The usual response to a logical argument is not, (3) You have convinced me to change my mind, or (2) I find a fallacy in your argument, but (1) I disagree with one of your premises.

So if A's first premise is like a stone wall that cannot be knocked down when B backs up against it, A's argument will be strong. If not, if A's premise can be challenged, then A will need another stone wall behind *it* to back *it* up. But then *that* wall will be challenged, so A will need another one to back *that* up, et cetera, et cetera, ad infinitum. Perhaps A can do this successfully each time his premises are challenged; but this is not an effective way for A to convince B, because somewhere in the chain of et ceteras, those who hear or read this argument will make the reasonable suggestion that since we cannot agree about principles, we should simply be civilized and agree to disagree, that is, be pro-choice.

Thus, pro-choicers say they are not pro-abortion but pro-choice, as agnostics say they are not anti-God, but anti-dogmatism, anti-certainty. And this seems most reasonable and civilized. How dare we be dogmatic? How narrow-minded for the pro-lifer to claim abortion is a clear evil rather than a "difficult issue"!

However, I have never heard this "pro-choice" argument made about genocide or rape or slavery or racism. Why? Obviously because everyone knows these to be evils so great and so clear that no civilized society should legalize them. Most people, even "pro-choicers" on abortion, would admit that they are not "pro-choice" on slavery, for instance. But that means admitting that it is possible to have *clear and certain knowledge* about the goodness or evil of some human acts, at least, if not about abortion. From that admission, it is fairly easy to argue that it is also possible to have clear and certain knowledge about the evil of abortion. For this reason, some of the most philosophically sophisticated pro-choicers are reluctant to admit the principle that it is possible to have clear and certain knowledge, objective and rational knowledge, about the goodness or evil of *any* human act. They tend to be moral relativists or subjectivists.

But even moral relativists are not usually total skeptics. They claim that we cannot know what good and evil are, but they do not usually claim that we cannot know what an apple is. Thus my strategy will be to try to lead them step by step from this most modest of assumptions. If you deny even this assumption, if you claim you do not even know what an apple is, then please remind me not to eat anything if I am invited to your house.

Tradition and common sense accept our premise that we know what an apple is. Almost no one doubted that we know what an apple is until quite recently. Even now, such doubts are found only among the "chattering classes" (philosophers, scholars, "experts", media mavens, professors, journalists, mind-molders). It is commonsensical to claim that we know what an apple is; that is precisely what makes this premise radical today among the "chattering classes". For in these circles, common sense is sometimes the most radical and uncommon sense. In an age when rebellion is the new orthodoxy, the old orthodoxy is the only remaining rebellion. Descartes noted that "there is no idea so absurd that it has not been seriously taught by some philosopher."

2. We *really* know what an apple *really* is

From the premise that "we know what an apple is", I move to my second principle, which is only an explication of the meaning of the first one: that we really know what an apple really is. If this is denied, then the first principle is made to walk the plank. It becomes "we know, but not really, what an apple is, but not really." Step Two says only, "Let us not nuance Step One out of existence. Let us not do a little demythologization dance, a sneaky side-step. Let us not say we believe in apples only as we believe in the Tooth Fairy."

3. We really know what some real things really are

And from this, I deduce the third principle, also as an immediate logical corollary, that we really know what some real things really are. This follows if we only add the minor premise that "an apple is some real thing."

Now that did not seem too much of a stretch, did it? Did it make you feel like a religious bigot, a dangerous fanatic, or a right-wing extremist to claim that when we say "This is an apple, not a cherry", we are not talking nonsense?

(I promised above not to use rhetoric *instead of* logic; I did not promise not to add a little sarcastic spice to the argument. People cannot eat pepper instead of steak, but they can eat steak either with or without pepper.)

The third principle, of course, is the repudiation of skepticism. The secret has been out since Socrates that skepticism is logically self-contradictory. To say "I do not know" is to say "I know I do not know." Socrates' wisdom was not skepticism. He was *not*, according to the Delphic oracle, "the only man in the world who knew that he did not know". He had knowledge. But he did not claim to have wisdom. He knew he was not wise. That is a different affair and is not self-contradictory.

All forms of general skepticism are self-contradictory, no matter how we twist and turn and dance. Do you know you do not know? Are you certain that we cannot be certain? Is it an objective fact that we cannot know objective fact? Is it only apparent that we know only appearances? Is it an absolute truth that we cannot know absolute truth? Is it universally true that we cannot know universal truth? Is it unchangeably true that truth is changeable? Is it only your private opinion that no one can know anything but private opinion? Is it only probable that all is only probable? Is the "fact" that truth is culturally relative culturally relative? Shall we dogmatically affirm that "you can't be dogmatic"? Shall we preach, "Papa, don't preach"? How long before adolescents masquerading as philosophers tire of this game?

Although skepticism as a philosophy is self-contradictory, skepticism as a *methodological attitude* may be sensible, perhaps even to the extent of Descartes' "universal methodic doubt". There are other methods. Socrates did not use the method of universal methodic doubt, as Descartes did. Instead, he began with a kind of universal methodic faith in what his dialogue partner claimed; then he examined this claim and usually found it logically wanting. Socrates treated ideas as innocent until proved guilty, whereas Descartes, trying to do philosophy by the scientific method, treated ideas as guilty until proved innocent. Neither of these two methodological starting points is self-evidently wrong, and you may characterize either one or both of them as "skeptical" in a purely practical sense. For Socrates, too, was famous for leaving no idea unquestioned and claimed that "the unexamined life is not worth living." But although skepticism may be practically productive as a beginning, as a method, it is self-destructive and self-contradictory as an end, as a philosophy.

We are going to argue about the "right to life" and about human rights in general. All arguing about rights, about right and wrong, about justice, presupposes the principle that we really know what some things really are. Unless we accept this principle, we cannot argue about anything at all—that is, about anything real, as distinct from arguing about arguing, and about words and attitudes. Without this principle we cannot be civilized and rational. We can talk about feelings without it, but we cannot talk about justice without it. We can have a reign of feelings—or a reign of terror—without it; but we cannot have a reign of law without it.

We can even argue about ideas without it, but not about real things. Ideas are in minds; real things are "outside" minds. Ideas are the means by which we know real things; ideas are not the things we immediately know. If all we know immediately are ideas, then we can never know which ideas are true and which are false, because we can know no real things to measure them by. (Locke, Berkeley, Hume, and Kant are wrong on this issue; and Socrates, Aristotle, and Aquinas are right.)

4. We know what human beings are

Our fourth principle is that we know what *we* are, that we know what human beings are. If we know what an apple is, surely we know what a human being is. For we are not apples.

We do not live as apples. We do not feel what apples feel, if they feel anything. We do not experience the existence or growth or life of apples. Yet we know what an apple is. (This was admitted, remember. Do we want to go back on this admission already?) All the more, then, we know what *we* are; for we have "inside information", privileged information, more and better data here.

We obviously do not have *total*, or even "adequate", knowledge of ourselves, or of an apple, or even of a flea. There is obviously more "stuff we don't know" in a human being than in an apple. But there is also more "stuff we do know". To claim that "we know what we are" is *not* to claim that we know *all* that we are, or even that we know *adequately*, or *completely*, or *with full understanding*, anything at all of what we are. We humans are an impossible, maddening, wonderful mystery, a tangle of living oxymorons. We are a mystery. But we also *know* this mystery. Knowledge and mystery are no more incompatible than eating and hungering for more.

5. We have human rights because we are human beings

We now apply our principles to the question of human rights. Our fifth principle is the indispensable, commonsensical basis for human rights. It is that we have human rights because we are human beings.

We have not yet said *what* human beings are (for example, do we have souls?) or what human rights are (for example, do we have a right to "life, liberty, and the pursuit of happiness"?), but only the simple point that we have *whatever* human rights we have because we are *whatever* it is that makes us human.

This certainly sounds innocent enough. But it implies a general principle. Let us call that our sixth principle: Morality is based on metaphysics.

6. Morality is based on metaphysics

Metaphysics means simply philosophizing about being, about reality. Our sixth principle means (again, commonsensically) that rights depend on reality, and our knowledge of rights depends on our knowledge of reality.

By this point in our argument, some are probably feeling impatient and others uneasy. The impatient ones are commonsensical people, uncorrupted by the chattering classes. They are saying, "Of course, of course. We know all of this. Get on with it. Get to the controversial stuff." Ah, but I suspect we began with the controversial stuff. For not all are impatient; others are uneasy. "Too simplistic", "Too dogmatic", "Not nuanced", "A complex issue"—do phrases like these leap to mind as shields to protect you from the spear you know is coming soon? Are you dancing? Have you lost your intellectual innocence already? Are you no longer willing to claim the simple human honor of knowing what an apple is, because if you do, you foresee that you will have to claim the fearful honor of knowing what a human baby is, and what an abortion is, and what you are if you approve this?

This little personal appeal is not an argument, just a question with a "Request for Ruthless Honesty" label attached. Socrates did that sort of thing, remember? But if you wish, you can disregard this personal appeal; the rest of the argument still stands.

The principle that "morality depends on metaphysics" means that *rights depend on reality*, that *what is right depends on what is*. Even if you say you are skeptical of metaphysics, we all do use the principle in all moral or legal arguments. For instance, in the current debate about "animal rights", some of us think that animals do have rights and some of us think they do not, but we all agree that if they do have rights, they have *animal* rights, not human rights, *because they are animals*, not humans. For instance, a dog does not have the right to vote, as humans do, *because* a dog is not a rational animal, as a human is. But a dog may have a right not to be tortured, or at least we may have an obligation not to torture it. Why? Because of what a dog *is*, and because we really know enough about what a dog really is: We really know that a dog feels pain as a tree does not. Dogs have feelings, unlike trees; and dogs do not have reason, like humans; that is why it is wrong to break a limb off a dog but it is not wrong to break a limb off a tree, and that is also why dogs do not have the right to vote but humans do.

Perhaps the very concept of "animal rights" extends the franchise too far, beyond humanity to other species. Perhaps there is some question as to whether the right not to be tortured inheres in a dog in the same way as the right not to be murdered inheres in a human being. Perhaps there is some question as to whether it is misleading to use the term "animal rights" at all, since animals are not moral agents, only moral patients. But even those who deny that there are any "animal rights" admit that there are human wrongs and that one of these is torturing dogs. A dog may have no right not to be tortured by a man, but it is certainly wrong for a man to torture a dog.

Those who deny that annuals have rights also use the same principle. They argue that animals do not have rights *because of what they are*: they are not free and rational agents, not persons, not *I*'s; therefore they are not moral agents. And only moral agents have rights. Whether this argument is right or not, my point is not to resolve the dispute about animal rights, but to note that both sides appeal to the same principle: that morality depends on metaphysics. Without that principle, there can be no moral argument.

Take another example: the handicapped have handicapped rights *because of what they are*: because they are handicapped. For instance, people in wheelchairs have the right to an elevator in a public buildings because they are handicapped and therefore need it. The rest of us do not have that right (even though an elevator would be a nice convenience for us) *because of what we are*: not handicapped in that way. (Each of us is handicapped in many other ways. We are *all* "the handicapped".) The underlying principle is always that rights depend on reality. In fact, I think the most basic principle of all morality is what I call the Three-R Principle: Right Response to Reality.

One more example: parents have parental rights *because of what they are*: parents. For example, they have the right to forbid their seventeen-year-old child with a valid driver's license to drive his car because he has been driving irresponsibly lately. Non-parents do not have that right because of what they are, or rather because of what they are not: they are not that child's parents.

In other words, since the essential principle of morality is the Three-R Principle, you cannot do morality without metaphysics. Metaphysics is simply sanity, living in reality, seeking and following reality as our objective standard. The alternative is insanity, living in unreality, in fantasy, "creating your own reality", as the New Age sophists say. You can do that when you write fiction, but not when you drive, or perform operations, or do anything else in the real world— like deciding whether or not to kill somebody or deciding whether or not there is somebody there to kill.

The main reason some people deny that morality must be based on metaphysics is that they say we do not really know what reality is, we only have opinions. They point out, correctly, that we are less agreed about morality than about science or about everyday practical facts. We do not differ about whether the sun is a star, or about whether we need to eat in order to live. But we do differ about things like abortion and capital punishment and animal rights.

But the very fact that we argue about it—this very fact that the skeptic points to as a reason for skepticism—is a refutation of skepticism. We do not argue about how we feel, about subjective things. You never hear an argument like this: "I feel great." "No! I feel terrible." All argument presupposes some commonly known and commonly agreed premises. One arguer tries to show that this premise entails one conclusion, while the other arguer tries to show that it does not, or that it entails an opposite conclusion; but if there is no common premise, then there can be no argument at all. The essence of argument consists of first identifying a common premise that both arguers agree is true, and then adding a second premise that takes you to a conclusion that you believe but your opponent does not.

For instance, both pro-choicers and pro-lifers usually agree that it is wrong to kill innocent persons against their will and that it is not wrong to kill parts of persons, like cancer cells. And both the proponents and the opponents of capital punishment usually agree that human life is a great value; that is why the proponent wants to protect the life of the innocent by killing convicted murderers and why the opponent wants to protect the life of even the murderer. They disagree about how to apply the principle that human life is valuable, but they both assume and appeal to the same principle. They both claim to know something real. They both base their morality on their metaphysics.

Many moral arguments are about an apparent conflict of rights. For instance, when do human rights trump animal rights? Is it right to cause pain in animals in order to find out something that might help to relieve pain in humans? Always, sometimes, or never?

Moral arguments can be phrased in language about "rights" *or* in language about "values", and they can usually be translated from one of those moral languages to another. For example, if we argue about whether it is right to kill an intruding thief in your house or only to maim him, we might ask: "What happens when your right not to be robbed bumps up against the thief's right not to be killed?" In terms of "values", the question might read: "How should we say the value of the thief's life and the value of your money are related in this situation?" Or when we argue about capital punishment, we can ask how the right of society to impose a punishment proportioned to the crime is related to the right to life of a killer. Does he give up his right to life by killing? If a society does not have secure prisons, does it have the right to kill killers before they kill more innocent victims? Or we can ask this last question in terms of values. For example, we can ask: If the society *does* have secure prisons, does the life of the killer have more value than the extra money and trouble it would take to keep him in prison for life? My point is not to solve any of these questions, but to note that whenever we raise such questions, whenever we address any moral questions, we presuppose a knowledge of reality.

All these examples are examples of both moral and legal arguments. Legal rights and moral rights, of course, are not the same; but they are closely connected. The reason why we make a law against murder (to take an obvious example) is because we think it is wrong. We make it legally wrong because we believe it is both morally wrong and publicly harmful. If we do not think a thing is morally wrong or publicly harmful at all, we do not make laws against it, even if it is privately harmful. For example, we do not make laws against hitting yourself, but we do make laws against hitting other people.

Moral right and wrong is a broader category than legal right and wrong, for we do not and cannot criminalize all immorality; but we do not ordinarily criminalize what is *moral*. If we do, that is a bad law and we try to change it. The very idea of good laws and bad laws, the very idea of judging and changing and improving laws, presupposes some "higher law" or moral standard by which we judge these man-made laws. If this is not so, if there is no such "higher law", or "natural law", then there was nothing *really* wrong with pro-slavery laws, or Nazi racist laws; we just did not *like* them, as we do not like cockroaches, so we destroyed them.

That is, if we had the power. To deny a real moral law is to base man-made law on power. And this is our next point:

7. The only alternative to rights based on metaphysics is rights based on might

We often disagree about how to apply moral principles, but I hope we do not disagree with the principle itself that human rights are possessed by human beings because of what they are, because of their being, and not because some other human beings have the power to enforce their will. That would be, literally, "might makes right." Instead of using might in the service of right, that would be pinning the label of "right" on the face of might; justifying force instead of fortifying justice.

Those are the only two possibilities: either might makes right or right makes might. To believe in a real moral law "higher" than man-made positive law is to believe that might must be justified by right; to disbelieve in such a "higher" law is to believe that might makes right, that "right" is only the label attached to the laws by those who had the might to make them.

These are the only two possibilities, no matter what the political power structure, no matter who or how many hold the power, whether it is a single tyrant, or a king, or an aristocracy, or a majority of the people, or the vague sentiment Rousseau called "the general will". The political form does not change the principle. A constitutional monarchy, in which the king and the people are subject to the same law, is a rule of law, not of power. A lawless democracy, in which the will of the majority is unchecked, is a rule of power, not of law. De Tocqueville pointed out, in *Democracy in America*, that democracy is not incompatible with totalitarianism (a "soft totalitarianism"). For democracy and totalitarianism are not two logically contradictory answers to the same question, but answers to two different questions. Democracy is an answer to the question: "*In whom* is the public power ultimately located?" And the answer is: "In the *demos*, the people at large." Totalitarianism is an answer to the different question: "*How much* power do the public authorities have?" And its answer is: "Total power, power unchecked by law." It is the rule of might, not right; of will, not reason. It is what the most powerful and harmful propaganda film of all time called *The Triumph of the Will*. (Remember? I hope so. And I hope you also remember that "those who do not remember the past are condemned to repeat it.")

Brave New World is a soft totalitarianism; *1984* is a hard one. The hard totalitarianisms of Fascism and Communism almost won the world, but the first is dead; the second is dying. But soft totalitarianism is flourishing. It is harder to topple than hard totalitarianism, for it does not use tanks and planes but universities and newspapers and movies. And "the pen is mightier than the sword."

It is flourishing in places like Holland, where people are given involuntary euthanasia for exactly the same reason the Nazi eugenics program started: those in power have decided that they possess "life unworthy of life". That is the alternative to metaphysics; that is "might makes right", even if it is in the name of "compassion", as it was in the case of the German doctors in the 1920s who first called for involuntary euthanasia.

If you believe that rights are based on reality, that morality is based on metaphysics, you will probably believe, as I do, that all humans have human rights because all humans are human. But if you deny that morality is based on metaphysics, a second possibility opens up: that only some have rights because those others who give them rights have willed it that way. Thus,

8. There are only two possibilities: either all have rights or only some have rights

These are the only options that are logically possible. If there are any human rights at all, then either all human beings have human rights or only some do. There is no third possibility.

The choice between these two options is obviously extremely important. But the *reason* for holding either one of these two philosophies of human rights is even more important than which one you hold.

Suppose you believe that all human beings have human rights. Do you believe that they all have human rights *because they all have human being*? Do you do metaphysics? Are human rights "inalienable" because they are inherent in human nature, in the human essence, in the human being, in what humans in fact are? As long as a society believes that, and practices it, it is secure against tyranny and the usurpation of rights.

Or do you believe that all human beings have human rights *only because some human beings say so*—for example, because it is the current consensus of the majority? In that case it is only because some human wills have declared that all human beings have human rights. Those in power have generously given rights to all. But then you are not secure against usurpation, for *whoever gives rights can revoke them*. If rights are not inalienable because they inhere in our very essence, they wobble at the whims of the wills of those who gave them. The same human wills who say today that all humans have rights may well say tomorrow that only some have rights.

You can believe either of these two philosophies, that all or only some have rights, for either of two reasons, because these rights are inherent in human nature or because the human wills of those in power say so. But there is more danger in a philosophy that believes the right thing for the wrong reason than there is in a philosophy that believes the wrong thing for the right reason. There is more danger in believing that all have human rights because some say so than there is in believing that only some have rights because only some have the full human essence. The United States Supreme Court, in the *Dred Scott* decision, said that Blacks were not persons but property, and thus runaway slaves had to be returned. This is absurd, but since that Supreme Court did not deny the principle that rights depend on reality, its absurdity was eventually seen and slavery was outlawed. It denied that all had rights, but not that rights were based on reality. But the same court, in *Planned Parenthood v Casey*, repudiated the principle that rights are based on any objective reality that we could know. In order to justify *Roe v Wade* and abortion, it claimed that "at the heart of liberty" is the right to define for oneself the meaning of life and the mystery of existence.

If you dare to base your beliefs on the facts, then even the silliest racism or elitism will eventually find the facts and face the facts and reform. But if you do not; if you do not accept the principle that morality is based on metaphysics, that rights are based on reality; if you shift the ground of rights to the human will—then you will continue to believe that all have rights only as long as you *want* to.

I now turn to the political dimension of this egalitarianism or universalism of human rights.

9. The relation between morality and society: Rights do not come from society

The issue that most critically and crucially divides Western civilization today, the issue whose resolution will decide the life or death of that civilization, is the origin and basis of morality. Is morality based on society, on political order? On popular consensus, in a democracy, or on the will of the dictator, in a dictatorship? Or is it the other way round? Are society and politics based on morality and to be judged by moral standards? Is there a higher law than the law of the state, or is the state God? Is there a God who justly judges the peoples, or is the voice of the people the voice of God (*vox populi, vox dei*)? Are human rights assigned by human wills and human societies, and therefore to be judged, reassigned, or subtracted by them? Or are human wills and human societies to be judged by inherent human rights?

The issue is embarrassingly simple (embarrassing to just one side): Moral absolutists believe in inherent rights, and moral relativists do not. If rights are not inherent and absolute, then they are invented by human wills and therefore possessed only by those human beings who are declared to have them—and those who have the power to do so make those declarations. It does not matter whether these are an aristocracy, a single monarch, a majority, or "the general will". Quality does not depend on quantity. The reason for rights is more important than how many have them and how many give them. "All men have rights only because all men give them" is still as unstable and untrustworthy as the human will, its final court of appeal. It can easily turn into "only some (the born) have rights because we in power now say so." In fact, this is exactly what has already happened in America.

My tenth point is not an essential step in my argument, and not a consequence strictly deduced from the previous point; it is only a political way of labeling the previous point, a political sidebar to it.

10. Extending the franchise to all is "good liberalism"

Forty years ago I was a liberal. Now I am a conservative. Yet I have not changed my position on anything. The label-makers have changed the labels.

Forty years ago, the politicians we called leftists, or liberals, or Democrats, were the ones who usually argued for equal rights (especially for the poor and disenfranchised) on the basis of the natural law, on the basis that political laws should be subject to moral laws. The politicians we called rightists, or conservatives, or Republicans, usually argued pragmatically, on the basis of economic efficiency. The same argument about principles is still going on today, but the labels have almost exactly changed places. When it is unborn children who are the poor and disenfranchised, those who argue for them on the basis of the natural law are called "right-wing extremists". (In mediaspeak, there is no such creature, in any possible world, as a "left-wing extremist.")

One of the greatest things about American democracy, I believe, is its continual growth in moral wisdom by extending the franchise: first to the poor as well as the rich (there used to be a property test for voting, so that only rich property owners had the franchise), then to women ("woman suffrage"), then to Blacks, by outlawing segregation as well as slavery. That is why I used to vote for Democrats and "liberals", as most Catholics did. For exactly the same reason, I now vote for Republicans and "conservatives". For they are the ones whose platform now supports extending the franchise to the most helpless class of people in the world, the unborn.

But even many Republicans are pro-abortion. Of course, they say they are not pro-abortion but pro-choice. They say they are "personally opposed but". I would like to give such politicians the "Pontius Pilate 'Personally Opposed to Crucifying the Innocent *But*' Award" for the biggest But.

What *is* "liberal" then? My eleventh point is an extension of the tenth, an explication of the label:

11. Liberalism entails traditionalism

Liberalism entails egalitarianism, and this entails extending the franchise, and this entails traditionalism, for traditionalism is "the democracy of the dead" as Chesterton called it: "extending the franchise not only to those disenfranchised by accident of birth but also by accident of death. Tradition counters the small and arrogant oligarchy of the living, that small minority who happen to be walking around the planet alive."

A reasonable traditionalism is not absolute, but pragmatic. Tradition is not infallible, but it should be given the benefit of the doubt. The onus of proof is on the radical. This is only reasonable. To take an example from Chesterton, suppose you are walking in the woods and suddenly come upon some strange structure that you can see no good use for. Should you tear it down since you do not understand its purpose, or should you let it be until you do understand its purpose and know that it is no longer needed? Obviously, the latter is more reasonable.

Traditions were made by human beings. Should not a venerable tradition be treated as innocent until proved guilty, like a human being? Tradition is a great collective human deed. I think it is reasonable that both people and their deeds should be treated as innocent until proved guilty. This applies to both the deed of abortion and the person aborted. So I admit that the onus of proof is on the pro-lifer to show why the deed of abortion is wrong and that the baby is a person. I shall do this below. But the onus of proof is also on the pro-choicer to show why the baby is guilty. No one has ever done that.

If it is reasonable to give the presumption of innocence to the great collective human deed of tradition, then the onus of proof must be on the pro-choicer, for tradition is pro-life.

Well, why *is* abortion wrong? I have accepted the onus of proof; what is my proof?

12. Abortion is wrong because the Golden Rule is right

Abortion is wrong because of the most simple, obvious, and universally accepted of all moral principles: the Golden Rule, "Do unto others what you would have them do unto you, and do not do unto others what you would not have them do unto you." Combine this principle, as one premise, with the fact that a human fetus is a fetal human, a human being, as the other premise, and you get the conclusion that abortion is wrong.

I will argue for the second premise shortly (point 13). My point here is the first premise, the Golden Rule.

Some people *want* to be killed. I will not address the morality of voluntary euthanasia here. But clearly, involuntary euthanasia is wrong. Clearly, there is a difference between imposing power on another and freely making a contract with another. A contract may still be a bad one, a contract to do a wrong thing; and the mere fact that the parties to the contract entered it freely does not automatically justify doing the thing they contract to do; but harming or killing another against his will, not by free contract, is clearly wrong. If that is not wrong, what is?

But that is what abortion is. The fetus does not want to be killed. It seeks to escape. (Did you see the film *The Silent Scream*? Did the media allow it to be shown? No. They will censor nothing except the most common operation in the world. You can see any perversity or obscenity you want, but you can never see a live abortion on any screen.)

13. Are some humans nonpersons?

The defender of abortion may admit the Golden Rule and the principle of universal, inherent human rights and yet deny them to unborn human beings. Philosophers who defend abortion sometimes make this move, saying that rights inhere only in persons and that we are not yet persons when we are at a fetal stage of development. So we need an argument for the nonexistence of nonpersons. The question we must now address is this: Are persons a subclass of humans, or are humans a subclass of persons?

The issue of distinguishing humans and persons comes up only for two reasons. One is the possibility that there are nonhuman persons, like extraterrestrials, elves, angels, gods, or the Persons of the Trinity. The other is the possibility that there are nonpersonal humans, unpersons, humans without rights.

Traditional common sense and traditional morality say that all humans are persons and have human rights. Modern moral relativism says that only some humans are persons, for only those who are given rights by others (that is, by those in power) have rights. Thus, if we have power we can "depersonalize" any group we will: Blacks, Jews, political enemies, fundamentalists, liberals, the unborn, the handicapped, or even infants. Peter Singer argues for a thirty-day waiting period during which parents can decide they do not want to keep, but want to destroy, the "product" they brought home from the hospital. Though most people are shocked by this proposal, the all-important question is: *Why not*? If the only answer is that our wills do not choose it because our emotions dislike it and our spontaneous, irrational consciousness has a prejudice against it—well, then, you can be sure that the media propaganda will soon soften all three of those obstacles. In fact, this has already happened. It is not an extremist prophecy of future doom, it is the simple story of recent history.

One way philosophers state the position that not all humans are persons and have rights is by attacking the traditional notion of universal human rights as "biologism" or "species-ism". They say that "*is* does not logically imply *ought*", they affirm an absolute "fact-value distinction", and consequently they claim that the fact of "membership in a biological species confers no rights." I have heard it argued that it is irrational to treat all humans as morally equal because we do not treat any other species in this way—for example, we do not assign equal rights to all mice. Some, we take good care of: those we adopt as pets or find useful in laboratory experiments. Some, we ignore: field mice, mice in the wild. And some, we kill: those that get into our houses and prove to be inconvenient to us. In this view, rights are assigned to all members of our own species only out of sentiment, prejudice, or tradition (the three being equated, as if nothing rational could be passed down by tradition). If we were mice (so the argument goes), we might assign a right to life to all mice, out of prejudice or loyalty (two concepts that are also often equated), but not to all humans. We would assign value to those humans who were valuable to us and assign a negative value to those who were not valuable to us and would declare it right to kill them. That is, if we had the power. When push comes to shove, moral relativism always turns out to be "might makes right."

And if "might makes right" does not disturb you, I know of no further argument that can persuade you. I think you are a bully, and you need the only thing you will respect: not an argument but a spanking.

We must finish up by formulating our argument, and the ways it can be met, by specifying:

14. Three pro-life premises and three pro-choice alternatives

There are three essential premises to the pro-life argument, and therefore three possible pro-choice rebuttals, depending on which premise is denied. To be pro-choice, you must deny at least one of them, because taken together they logically entail the pro-life conclusion. But there are three very significantly different pro-choice positions, depending on which of the three pro-life premises is targeted.

The first premise is scientific, the second is moral, and the third is legal.

1. The scientific premise is that *the life of the individual member of every animal species*, and therefore also of the human species, *begins at conception*, when a genetically new and genetically complete individual first comes into existence. This truism was taught in all biology

textbooks in America that were written before abortion was legalized, in 1972, but not by most of those that were written after 1972. Yet the new textbooks did not appeal to a single new scientific discovery to justify their change. Draw your own conclusions from those data.

So the first premise of the pro-life argument is that all humans are human, whether they are dying humans, or old humans, or mature humans, or young humans, or infantile humans, or fetal humans, or embryonic humans.

2. The moral premise is that *all humans have the right to life* because all humans are human. All humans have human nature, have the human essence, are essentially equal. The universal right to life is a deduction from the most obvious of moral rules, the Golden Rule, or Justice, or Equality. Since you do not want others to kill you against your will, you ought not to kill others against their will. It is just not fair, not just.

3. The legal premise is that *the law must protect the most basic human rights.* If all humans are human, and if all humans have a right to life, and if the law must protect human rights, then the law must protect the right of all humans to life.

If all three premises are true, the pro-life conclusion follows. From the pro-life point of view, there are only three reasons anyone can be pro-choice: scientific ignorance, moral ignorance, or legal ignorance—in fact, appalling scientific ignorance, ignorance of a scientific fact so basic that nearly everyone knows it; or appalling moral ignorance, ignorance of the most basic of all moral laws; or appalling legal ignorance, ignorance of one of the most basic of all the functions of the law.

But though the three kinds of ignorance are all appalling, they are not equally appalling. Scientific ignorance, if it is honest, if it is really ignorance rather than ignoring, is pitiable but not always morally blameworthy. You do not have to be wicked to be stupid. If it is possible to believe sincerely that an unborn baby is only "a group of cells" or "potential life" (What is that? The undead?), then it is possible to believe sincerely you are not killing a human being when you have an abortion. (But why, then, do most mothers who abort have such terrible dreams? And why do most of them deeply regret it when they are older and wiser?)

Most pro-choice arguments during the first two decades after *Roe v Wade* was passed disputed the scientific premise of the pro-life argument. Perhaps this was usually dishonest rather than honest ignorance, but perhaps not; and at least it did not directly deny the essential moral principle in premise two. But pro-choice arguments today increasingly do just that. Perhaps pro-choicers perceive that they have no choice here, for scientific facts are not deniable, as moral principles are. Whatever the reason, it is a vast sea-change, for the camel of moral relativism has gotten not just his nose under the tent but his torso.

I think most people do not want to think or argue about abortion logically, because they instinctively see that the only way to remain pro-choice is to abort their reason and conscience first. I repeatedly hear pro-choicers themselves admit that abortion is not about babies but about "quality of life" or "lifestyles", which is usually a euphemism for sex. It makes sense, after all, for the only reason a woman wants abortion is as backup birth control, and birth control is the demand to have sex without having babies. If storks brought babies, Planned Parenthood would be out of business. Perhaps a pro-choicer is smart enough to see that the only way to justify his or her rejection of sexual virginity and honor is a rejection of intellectual virginity and honor; that you need to lose your intellectual innocence to justify losing your moral innocence. But I cannot prove this offensive suspicion, so I can only dare you to ask yourself, quietly and honestly, whether you *know* it is false, or only *need* it to be false.

My last argument, a kind of addendum or extra, is:

15. The argument from skepticism

I think the most likely response to my argument will be the charge of dogmatism. How dare I pontificate with such certitude and imply that all who disagree are either mentally or morally challenged? All right, then, here is an argument even for the skeptic, who would not even agree with my very first premise that we know what an apple is, that we really know what some real things really are, that we can base morality on metaphysics. (Have you noticed that it is only after you are pinned against the wall and have to justify something like abortion that you become a skeptic?)

It is fashionable to appeal to such skepticism to justify being "pro-choice": Since we do not know with certainty when human life begins, the argument goes, we should not impose restrictions.

The simple answer to this argument is to demand a reason why it is more restrictive to give life than to take it; why allowing abortion does not impose a more severe and violent restriction on its victim than forbidding abortion does. And the only possible answer is that we know that the human fetus is not a person with rights; the answer presupposes that the mother is more human, or more valuable, than her unborn child. But that presupposes not skepticism but knowledge: that we *know* that abortion's victim is not a human person with rights equal to that of the mother. So this is not an argument from skepticism but from anti-skepticism.

To put this last argument in a more purely logical form, let us suppose that not a single principle of this essay is true, beginning with the first one. Let us suppose that we do not even know what an apple is, much less what an abortion is or what the thing it kills is. Even then abortion is unjustifiable. Why?

Let us assume, not a dogmatic skepticism (which is self-contradictory), but a skeptical skepticism. Let us be skeptical even about skepticism. Let us assume that we do not know whether a fetus is a person or not, and that we do not know whether or not we can know that. We still know two things by formal logic alone, without presupposing any knowledge of the real world at all. First, we know that either the fetus is or it is not a human person with a right to life, just as we know that it is either a Martian or not, either hairless or not, and so on. We may not know which it is, but we know that everything must be either x or not x. And the second thing we know is that we either do or do not know what it is. So either the fetus is or is not a human person, and either the person who justifies abortion knows, or does not know, what the fetus is. So there are only four logically possible situations:

1. the fetus is a human person and we know that;
2. the fetus is a human person and we do not know that;
3. the fetus is not a human person and we do not know that;
4. the fetus is not a human person and we know that.

There can be no fifth possibility, not because of what a fetus is or because of what abortion is or because of what our knowledge is or because of what an apple is (we do not have to presuppose any factual knowledge of objective reality at all; we can be total skeptics), but simply because of the inescapable and undeniable laws of logic. (Technically, they are "the law of non-contradiction" and "the law of excluded middle".) It is literally impossible for anyone ever to think contrary to these laws; they are the laws intrinsic to all thought. Even the Supreme Court cannot revoke the Law of Non-Contradiction (although that might be news to some of them).

Now what is abortion in each case?

In case no. 1, where the fetus is a human person and you know that, abortion is murder. It is the deliberate killing of what you know to be an innocent human person. No amount of pro-choice protest about how this word hurts them and imperils civil discussion can change that fact.

In case no. 2, where the fetus is a human person but you do not know that, abortion is manslaughter. It is like driving over a man-shaped overcoat in the street at night, or shooting into a bush that may contain your fellow hunter, or fumigating a building with toxic chemicals without being sure the building is fully evacuated. You do not know that there is a person there, but you do not know that there is not, either, and it just so happens that there *is* a person there, and you kill that person. You cannot plead ignorance. True, you did not know there was a person there, so you did not intend deliberate murder. But you did not know there was not, either, so your act was literally the height of irresponsibility. And that is the act pro-choicers want to allow anyone to choose.

In case no. 3, where the fetus is not a person but you do not know that, abortion is just as irresponsible as it was in the previous case. You ran over the overcoat, shot into the bush, or fumigated the building without knowing that there were no persons there. You were lucky; there were not. But you did not know and you did not care. You were just as irresponsible. You cannot legally be charged with murder or even with manslaughter, because no man was slaughtered, but you can and should be charged with criminal negligence.

Only in case no. 4, where the fetus is not a person and you know that, is abortion morally reasonable, responsible, and permissible. But note carefully that what makes case no. 4 permissible is not merely the fact that the fetus is not a person but also your knowledge of that fact, your overcoming of skepticism. *So skepticism cannot count for abortion but only against it.* Only if you are *not* a skeptic can abortion be moral. Only if you are *certain* that there is no person in the overcoat, the bush, the building, or the womb may you drive, shoot, fumigate, or abort.

This undercuts even the weakest, silliest, and least honest escape: to pretend you do not even know what an apple is just so that you have an excuse for claiming that you do not know what an abortion is.

A concluding plea

I hope someone can show me where I have gone wrong in my argument. Which step is illogical? Or perhaps you want to say the silliest thing of all, that the very laws of logic are illogical, that it is true that there is no truth, that two contradictory propositions can both be true at the same time? Do you want to deny the validity of all arguments just so that you can escape this one?

I honestly wish that some day some pro-choice thinker would show me one argument that proved that the victim of abortion was *not* a human person, with a right to life. That would save me and millions of other pro-lifers enormous grief, worry, effort, time, work, and money. But until that time, I will keep arguing because it is what I do, as a philosopher. It is my weak version of a mother shouting and screaming that something terrible is happening: babies are being slaughtered. I will do this because "the only thing necessary for the triumph of evil is that good men do nothing."

That is certainly sufficient reason for working passionately for the pro-life cause. But there is an even more momentous reason, the ultimate reason, the ultimate court of appeal if you believe the words of the man nearly everyone admits was at least a moral expert, a wise man, and a truth teller, and the man Christians believe was God incarnate: "Truly, truly, I assure you, whatever you do to one of the least of these, my littlest ones, you do to me."

Historical Postscript

The company that today manufactures RU-486, the abortion pill, is Roussel-Uclaf, which is a subsidiary of Hoechst, and Hoechst is a spinoff of I. G. Farben, the company that manufactured Zyklon-B, the gas the Nazis used to murder the Jews in Auschwitz.[1] Some might call this fact "ironic". I would call it eerie.

I also find it eerie that Planned Parenthood, the world's largest abortion provider and the world's most powerful pro-abortion propaganda machine, has never repudiated its founder Margaret Sanger's enthusiastic embracing of Nazi eugenics. She had a personal friendship with some of the high-ranking Nazi doctors and generals who wrote articles for her in her journal, advocating killing the "biologically unfit" out of "compassion". Later, the targeted population was expanded to include the racially and politically "unfit". Planned Parenthood has never repudiated any of her ideas. She was a racist if anyone ever was, and a deliberate liar. Her admitted strategy was to con Black ministers in America unwittingly to aid her cause of reducing or even eliminating this "inferior" race step by step, by persuading Blacks to limit their population by contraception, sterilization, and abortion. Her principle was: "more babies from the fit, less from the unfit". Planned Parenthood still targets Blacks and

[1] William Brennan, Ph.D., "An Unbroken Legacy of Corporate Chemical Warfare against the Vulnerable", *Celebrate Life* (Jan.–Feb. 1998), pp. 40–42.

Hispanics disproportionately. Today, the American Library
Association, which claims to be against censorship and will
not censor even child pornography, does censor one book:
a scholarly, factual, documented exposé of Margaret Sanger
and Planned Parenthood, *Grand Illusion*, by George Grant.
This is the one book in print on the subject of the history
of Planned Parenthood that tells the whole truth, and the
one book that you will not find in American "public"
libraries.

Sometimes I think we are no longer living in a free country with a free press. Why should we expect to? How naïve
can we be? Our establishment is pro-killing; why should we
be surprised to find it pro-censorship? Why should we expect those who are anti-life to be pro-truth? They have something terrible to hide; why are we surprised that they hide
it? Why would people without consciences that condemn
murder have consciences that condemn lying, especially lying about their murders? Why would they not love a morality whose only sin is "judgmentalism"?

I hope this dark thought of mine is wrong. But it is logical. Once you admit the principle that some people grant
the right to life to others, it follows that they can remove it
from others as they will; and if the right to life from some,
why not the right to truth from others?

One of America's most famous thinkers, Justice Oliver
Wendell Holmes, shared much of Planned Parenthood's philosophy. Here is what he wrote in 1927, in a Supreme Court
decision justifying the State of Virginia's compulsory sterilization law:

> We have seen more than once that the public welfare may
> call upon the best citizens for their lives. It would be strange
> if it could not call upon those who already sap the strength
> of the state for these lesser sacrifices, often not felt to be

such by those concerned, in order to prevent our being swamped with incompetence. It is better for all the world if instead of waiting to execute degenerate offspring for crime, or to let them starve for their imbecility, society can prevent those who are manifestly unfit from continuing their kind. The principle that sustains compulsory vaccination is broad enough to cover cutting of the Fallopian tubes. (Justice Oliver Wendell Holmes, U.S. Supreme Court, 1927 [274 US 200])

This is exactly the reasoning of the landmark book by German doctors, *Life Unworthy of Life*, that was the beginning of Nazi eugenics. The argument was from "compassion" on those deemed "unfit", those "lives unworthy of life". That is why, in *The Thanatos Syndrome*, Walker Percy says that "compassion led to the death camps." In fact, in *Mein Kampf* Hitler mentioned *American* eugenics programs as a model for what he wanted in Germany (see *New Oxford Review*, January 2001).

Traditional moral absolutism (the belief that there are some moral absolutes such as "Thou shalt not murder") is usually presented today, by the "liberal" mind-molding establishments, as oppressive and driven by power; and moral relativism is presented as "liberal" or liberating, as driven by compassion and principle. This is a perfect example of what Hitler called a "Big Lie".

And to counter it, here is a "Big Truth", from Mussolini:

Everything I have said and done in these last years is relativism by intuition.... If relativism signifies contempt for fixed categories and men who claim to be the bearers of an objective, immortal truth ... then there is nothing more relativistic than Fascistic attitudes and activity.... From the fact that all ideologies are of equal value, that all ideologies are mere fictions, the modern relativist infers that everybody has the right to create for himself his own ideology and to attempt to enforce it with all the energy of which he is capable.[2]

Eerily reminiscent of the "mystery" passage in *Planned Parenthood v Casey*, is it not? In order to justify the right of some (mothers) to kill others (their unborn children), the Court asserted the most radical principle of moral relativism; to justify playing God over life, we assert the right to play God over truth, the right to create meaning, the right to be the Author of truth. If the claim to have Author's rights over truth itself is not authoritarianism, what is?

To see how far we have come since 1776, to set side by side the birth of America with the death of America, compare this passage with the first sentence of our first document, the Declaration of Independence, probably the most well known and beloved quotation in American history: "We hold these truths to be self-evident: that all men are created equal, that they are endowed by their Creator with certain inalienable rights; that among these rights are life, liberty, and the pursuit of happiness."

America's Civil War was about liberty. Our current abortion war is about the even more fundamental right, life. Abraham Lincoln's Gettysburg Address asked whether the Civil War dead have "died in vain" and left the question to be answered by "us, the living". We are the living, and we are now deciding this question, the central question of World War Three, the war between the Culture of Death and the Gospel of Life.

---

[2] Benito Mussolini, *Diuturna*, pp. 374–77, quoted by Helmut Kuhn, *Freedom Forgotten and Remembered* (Chapel Hill, N.C.: University of North Carolina Press, 1943), pp. 17–18.

Three natural rights, three enemies, and three wars

The Declaration of Independence lists three fundamental and inherent human rights: life, liberty, and "the pursuit of happiness". The original text had "property" as the third right. (It was probably changed by a rewrite adman whose descendents two centuries later got rich in Hollywood and Madison Avenue, and whose ancestors go back to the Garden of Eden, where the world's oldest profession, advertising, was invented: "See this apple? You need this apple. It only costs one soul. Eat it. Until you do, you do not really know what an apple is.")

These three rights—life, liberty, and property—are in a natural hierarchical order: life is the foundation for liberty, and liberty is the foundation for property. For dead people cannot be free, and slaves cannot have their own property, because they *are* property.

All three rights have been under attack in modern times.

Personal property was attacked by Communism, which succumbed in 1989 in the U.S.S.R. without a drop of blood being spilled.

Freedom was attacked by slavery, which succumbed in 1863 in America after many drops of blood were spilled.

Life in the womb is currently under attack by abortion, and life at the other end of the life cycle by euthanasia. This third enemy will inevitably succumb too, for it is just as contrary to human nature as Communism or slavery are. But it has not yet been decided when it will succumb, how many victims it will take with it, and whether its fall will be bloody or unbloody.

The war we are in today is a continuation of the age-old war of the forces of life against the forces of death. To see where we are in this story, to get a sense of historical perspective, let us review three of the most crucial and spectacular battles in this war.

Battle no. 1: Almost four thousand years ago, the Culture of Death reigned among the Caananites, who sacrificed their children to a bloodthirsty god named Moloch. Newborn babies were thrown into his fires, and children were made to commit suicide by walking through fire, in a valley called Ge Hinom, or Gehenna. When God's chosen people, entering their Promised Land, saw this infanticide, they recognized it as a more-than-human evil, as the work of demons. Their God, the Prince of Peace, commanded them to exterminate this culture totally, down to its sheep and cattle. After they had done this, they would not set foot in that cursed valley and used it only to burn garbage. The fires never went out, day or night (no matches). Gentle Jesus used that place— Gehenna—as his image for Hell. Jesus was not tolerant of the devil's intolerance toward innocent human lives—his little ones.

Battle no. 2: About five hundred years ago, a strikingly similar Culture of Death reigned in Aztec Mexico. Some historians estimate that one out of every three children in that great culture were ritually sacrificed to their blood-thirsty and demanding god with the unpronounceable name— exactly the same proportion of children conceived in America who are aborted today. (In Russia, the proportion is even higher; the average Russian woman aborts three of her children in her lifetime.) The Aztec priests were extremely efficient at gouging the living heart out of the victim with a stone knife, then throwing the corpse down the great stone steps of their pyramids to be eaten by wild animals. It took only fifteen seconds per victim, and the victims lined up for slaughter in four straight lines as far as the eye could see, one in each direction of the compass. One festival in the capital saw twenty-eight thousand children killed, over a period of eight days. When Cortez and his conquistadors saw this, they

also, like the ancient Jews, recognized it as the work of demons. Cortez scuttled all but one of his ships, and three hundred Spanish soldiers fought all day for thirty days and
prevailed against odds of over ten thousand to one. Cortez
stopped the human sacrifice and paved the way for thirteen
Franciscan priests to come and evangelize this people. In following years there were five million conversions, aided by
the miracle of Juan Diego and Our Lady of Guadalupe. Cortez
was not a saint, but his intolerance of the devil's intolerance
to human lives lined up with Yahweh and Jesus.

Battle no. 3: In 1941, Hitler's death machine had conquered nearly all of Europe and was about to invade England. Unlike Chamberlain, Churchill was not tolerant of
Hitler's intolerance and vowed to fight the Nazis on the
beaches, to fight them in the hedgerows, never, never, never
to give up. It was indeed England's finest hour. And Irish
soldiers fought alongside the English in that hour, so unlike
the hour of the famine in the nineteenth century or the Trou-
bles in the twentieth. America then shared that "finest hour".
But today the Culture of Death has returned, and England
and America have succumbed to its primary sacrament. Today it is not England but Ireland that is the last outpost in
Europe of freedom and life. Let us pray that Ireland does not
choose to be tolerant of the devil's intolerance to innocent
human life. Thomas Cahill has chronicled the eighth century story of *How the Irish Saved Civilization* in his delightful
book by that title. But now they must do it again. For the
same enemy, lusting after the same baby's blood, but using
the subtler weapons of words and laws, must again be recognized and defeated as he was by the Jews, and by Jesus,
and by Cortez, and by Churchill. Then it was England, now
it is Ireland who stands alone, who fights them in the newspapers and in the ballot boxes, and never, never, never gives

up. And when the barbarism ends, and the fog clears, and the world sees what they did, they will say of Ireland, "this was their finest hour."

For this war is not against Germany, or against England, but against principalities and powers, against the spiritual powrs of wickedness on high. It is the war of the god of death against the God of Life, of Antichrist against Christ, the Beast against the Lamb, Moloch the eater of children's hearts against the children. It is time to remember Moses' last words: Choose life. It is time to be both pro-choice and pro-life by choosing life.

Since I have dared to be so concrete as to speak of *gods*, and not just abstract *goods*, we need to clear up a common misunderstanding about religion and politics. Am I advocating theocracy?

The God Connection

If we say that we have been "endowed by our Creator with certain inalienable rights", do we say that no atheist can be a good citizen? No. That we have to believe in God if we are to believe in universal inalienable rights? No. Why not, if God is in fact the one who gives us these inalienable rights? After all, the only alternative givers of rights are other human beings, and then we are back in moral relativism and "might makes right." Is it not true, as both Dostoyevsky the Christian and Sartre the atheist say, that "if there is no God, then everything is permissible"?

Yes, it is true. But we do not have to know that it is true in order to know that all men have inherent, inalienable rights. Just as a scientist can know physical laws without knowing the Maker of these laws, and just as the psychologist can know much about human nature without knowing the God who created it in his own image, so the moralist or the politician or the lawyer can know God's moral effects, the moral law, the natural law, without knowing its ultimate cause, the divine Lawgiver. For just as physical laws were designed by God to be natural laws, inherent in the very nature of the material universe, so moral laws were designed by God to be natural laws too, laws inherent in the very nature of man. In morality as in science, you can know the effect even without knowing the cause; you can trace the line of causality back just so far and no farther, stopping short of the First Cause. And a nation can be based on such natural laws whether or not it is based on a religious recognition of the ultimate Lawgiver.

Wherever human rights ultimately come from, they come proximately from human nature, not from human wills. They are inherent, not assigned. Even God himself did not assign them in an external, willful, legalistic way. It is not because God wills justice and charity that they are good. Rather, God wills them because they are good in themselves. (Euthyphro, Ockham, Luther, Calvin, and Descartes were wrong; Socrates, Cicero, Augustine, Aquinas, Hooker, Johnson, and C. S. Lewis were right on that point.) Good things are inherently good, for God as well as for man; for they are of the very nature of God, whose essential name is not Power but Goodness. But we are so depraved that we make "Almighty" his first name and "Good God" a swear word. We need to be reminded, by Dostoyevski, that "God is not in strength but in truth."

II

Why We Fight:
A Pro-Life Motivational Map

A confession of fifteen motives that fuel pro-life work

Pro-choice people would like to know the answer to the question in that title. Most of them do not understand us, some of them do not understand *why* they do not understand us, and some of them do not even understand *that* they do not understand us. Some want to understand us only to fight against us more effectively, and some want to understand us because they have some lingering doubts about whether we are as wrong as they thought we were, whether it just might be possible that we are "onto something". So for their sake, it is necessary for us to be very clear and candid about ourselves as well as our cause; about our private motives as well as our public reasons and arguments; about why we fight this fight.

This confession is also necessary for our sake. For if we are unclear about this motive, this moving principle, this source of our energy, or if the source is too shallow, it will dry up, and we will weaken, and give up, and lose.

So I asked myself the title question and demanded a complete, and completely honest, answer. And I came up with not one but fifteen motives. I shall list them in no particular order, except that I move (for the most part) from the more abstract to the more concrete, the more general to the more particular, and save the best till last.

These are subjective, personal, psychological motives, not objective, impersonal, universally valid rational arguments. My intention was to keep arguments out of this chapter and personal motivation out of Chapter One. However, the two are connected: arguments can spur motives. So I will not totally succeed in my intention to segregate these two things here, just as I did not do so in Chapter One either. This ambivalence is one of the things that comes out most strongly, and unavoidably, in most lived conversations on the subject, and it permeates the dialogue in chapter three of this book, where the two are deliberately combined.

1. Meaning

We fight for life, first, because of the truth of what Viktor Frankl discovered in Auschwitz and made the main point of his great little book *Man's Search for Meaning*: that every human being's deepest need in life is a meaning, a purpose, a cause, a reason to live and work and fight and suffer and die. Without this, nothing suffices; with this, anything is endurable. Frankl quotes Nietzsche's dictum, "A man can endure almost any *how* if only he has a *why*." Even Freud admitted two psychological absolutes, two universal needs: love and work, meaningful work, purposive work.

Mothers are obviously involved in a tremendously meaningful work. Every stage of motherhood—courtship, marriage, getting pregnant, each stage of pregnancy, childbirth, and the trillions of things involved in a lifetime of raising children after birth—is loaded with meaning and purpose. And that meaning is *life*, more life, better life, future life. Mothering is excruciatingly demanding work, both before and after birth; but it is wonderfully meaningful work. Being a mother is perhaps the single hardest job in the world, probably the least appreciated job in the world, and certainly the most important job in the world. (The fact that it is unappreciated is a chilling indicator of our culture's deep inner illness.)

There are other demanding jobs that are also attractive because they are so obviously meaningful, such as that of a police officer, firefighter, social worker, or nurse. These jobs are all hard work and some are dangerous, but they all have a strong and clear sense of purposiveness. They help people to overcome very clear and present dangers. They make life meaningful: a story, not an episode.

Death is a very clear and present danger for unborn children in our culture. The womb, by nature the safest place in the world, has become the most dangerous and lethal place in the world. One out of every three persons who enter it leave it dead within nine months. Is there any other place on this planet more lethal except gas chambers and electric chairs? If we can contribute even a little bit, even indirectly, to saving a few small and unseen human beings from death, then in these small ways we shall have made our lives very meaningful.

2. Obligation

Second, it is not only a meaning but a moral obligation, a duty. I think all pro-lifers feel this. It is not an option, it is a necessity. It is not an obligation to be a firefighter or a social worker, or even a mother. But it is an obligation to fight to defend innocent human lives when they are under attack. It is not an "ideal" or a "value"; it is an "ought". How can we live with ourselves if we simply stand by while a legal holocaust happens around us in our own "civilization"?

There were many other holocausts in this century of genocide that has just ended: against Armenians by the Turks,
against the Jews by Hitler, against political enemies by
Stalin and Mao, and on the "killing fields" of Cambodia
and Rwanda. These ended, because they were dependent
on unstable political regimes and military actions; but
the abortion holocaust is not ending, and it has spread
almost globally. Ireland and the Islamic nations are almost
the only ones that have refused to take part in it. It is
not dependent on nation or culture. It is not merely political or military. We cannot wait for the marines to come
over the hilltop to save us. We are the marines. If we do
not do something, no one will. We must fight because we
feel it is a crime against conscience to stay home from the
polls when thousands of polite little Hitlers are running for
office.

3. Honesty

In addition to the personal satisfaction of working for a good
purpose, and the moral rightness of obeying conscience, there
is also the intellectual honesty of facing the truth.

Two philosophies are at war in our world. They are clearly
distinguished by how they define four words: "truth", "honesty", "realism", and "reality". The first philosophy, the oldest one, says that truth is objective and universal and that we
can know it and that we are all obligated to live by it. In this
philosophy, "honesty" means seeking this objective truth; and
"realism" means conforming our thoughts and lives to this
reality; and "reality" includes a real right and wrong. In the
second philosophy, the typically modern (or "postmodern")
one, "truth" is subjective, "honesty" means shamelessness,
"realism" means cynicism, and "reality" means what we can

kick. America was founded on the first philosophy and is foundering upon the second.

How many times have we not heard the favorite slogan of subjectivism, "What right do you have to impose your values on me?" As if "values" were personal property like shoes and could be "imposed" on minds as shoes are imposed on squashed ants.

"What right do you have to impose your values on me?" really means "It's really not right to tell me that some things really are not right." That is not only logically self-contradictory, it is morally self-contradictory, or hypocritical. For it means committing the very sin you are preaching against. It means imposing your personal value system of moral relativism on others. This is not just logical weakness but moral dishonesty, hypocrisy. ("Hypocrisy" does not mean "not practicing what you preach"; it means "not believing what you preach". It means not moral weakness—that is common to all of us—but moral dishonesty.) But I suspect it is very hard to be honest when you are pro-abortion, for honesty means facing facts, and it is very hard to face three facts about abortion: (1) exactly what it does, what it is; (2) what its unborn victim is; and (3) what its adult victim suffers for the rest of her life.

Even if I knew nothing about the substantive issue between pro-choicers and pro-lifers, even if I were an extraterrestrial, I think I would be appalled by the way the debate is being conducted; by the dishonesty of the pro-choice media establishment. I would ask questions like these:

Why do we hear the pro-choice message from dozens of TV sitcoms and specials but never the pro-life message, except on private religious stations?

Why are there dozens of pro-choice movies but no pro-life movies? (*Alfie* was the last one.)

Why do the teachers in our society have such a radically different philosophy on this issue than the students? Why is America the least egalitarian society on earth on the most important and controversial issue of our day?

Why do only 3% of media leaders believe what 82% of Americans in general believe, namely, that abortion is in some sense wrong and in some way should be discouraged?[1] Why have our biology textbooks been changed? (See page 35.)

Why is it so hard to get a pro-choice intellectual (there are plenty) to debate a pro-lifer?

I think we know why.

4. Patriotism

A fourth reason we fight is the love of our country.

Would it not be great to be able to feel moral pride for America again instead of shame?

But what can one little citizen do? There are two options. First, you can just throw up your hands in despair, play the prophet of doom, and say "I told you so" as you watch this spiritual spider, swollen with the blood of holy innocents, dragging America into the same web into which it dragged the Caananites, the Romans, and the Aztecs. Or you could remember that America is *your* country, and that it was built by the sacrifices of your ancestors. Our country is, in a remote but real sense, our extended family. When your family is in distress, you do not abandon them, you rescue them. You do what you can; you do not say, "Oh, well, what can you do?"

When war breaks out between life and death, you do not go AWOL. You choose life. When death conquers great expanses of territory, you do not leave the battlefield. That

---

[1] See the Wirthlin Institute poll, Baltimore, Md., 1992.

territory is *your* territory, and your family's. If you have any honor or respect for your family, your ancestors, and the precious gifts they lived and died to give us, you will fight to defend these gifts.

The weapons we use are not those of our enemy. We use nonviolent resistance because we fight not to kill but to heal. But we fight. We fight with spiritual weapons because the battle is a spiritual battle, between the old "sanctity of life ethic", which made America great, and the new "quality of life ethic", which is making Americans dead. Dead physically if your quality-of-life index does not make it, and dead spiritually if you make peace with this killer.

5. Civilization

We fight to save not just America but civilization, grandiose as that sounds.

A generation or two ago, we divided the world into three "worlds": the "first world" of Western democracies, the "second world" of the Communist states, and the "third world" of the undeveloped nations. The three worlds are becoming two as Communism is dying, and they are becoming one as undeveloped nations develop. And they are developing into the image of America. America is putting its stamp increasingly on the whole world, for it is the world's only superpower, culturally as well as economically and militarily. It is up to us to choose whether the stamp of the whole world looks more like Lincoln or Lennon (I mean John Lennon, not Vladimir Lenin, but their philosophies had much in common), more like *the* Madonna or Madonna. (What a difference a "the" makes!)

Our civilization, like our country, is our family. It is not our eternal home, but it *is* our temporal home, our "home away from home". Western civilization is not the Church, but it used to be called "Christendom"; it is not the Kingdom of Heaven, but it has been God's providentially chosen instrument to house temporarily much of his Kingdom throughout most of Christian history. It is not necessary, but it is good.

The present "culture war", the spiritual war between the Gospel of Life and the Culture of Death, is the greatest war in our history. It is a world war far deeper and more extensive than World War II. It is deeper because it attacks life itself, body and soul, at its root and origin. It is more extensive because it spreads over the whole world like a cancer. Even if we had lost World War II and Hitler had won, and had conquered and occupied America, we would have survived, as Denmark and Norway and Holland survived. There probably would have been a horrible price to pay in bloody bodies, of course. But the Nazis did not conquer the souls of these subjugated peoples. That is why they rose again. Wars are won, in the final analysis, by spirit and lost by lack of spirit. That is why Communism fell under its own weight (or weightlessness). The only earthly power that defeated ancient Rome was Rome herself. The barbarians just picked up the pieces. And the only power that will defeat America is America.

It is faith that wins wars. (Read Hebrews 11.) Faith is not a feeling or a concept; it is an act, in fact a lifetime of acts. Faith literally moves mountains, for faith works. Faith without works is dead, and so are works without faith. That is why, just one generation after we defeated the greatest military power in history, we lost to Ho Chi Minh. World War II was a work of faith; Viet Nam was a work without faith.

America is not doomed. The patient is not dead, only comatose. It can revive. Revivals have happened. It happened to ancient Israel, under Josiah, and to China, after Confucius. Nations have had saviors and heroes: Bolivar, Garibaldi, Walesa and Wojtyla, Washington and Lincoln. The "Great Awakening" in the nineteenth century began in America and then spread to Europe. Marx is wrong: history is not predetermined. One individual can move millions. Free individuals can move history, as they move great stones: with long, slow, hard, committed, united pressure.

6. Families

The single most essential foundation and building block of all human civilization is families. And this is our sixth reason for fighting for the lives of unborn children: to save the institution founded by God to be the most fundamental institution on earth. The family is more fundamental than either the state or the church, for there can be no state or church without the family.

That is why pro-lifers are so concerned with issues like homosexual "marriage": not out of fear of homosexuals or out of loathing for homosexuality, but to preserve the family against a destruction of its very nature by "redefining" it to include two or more cohabiting individuals of the same sex. It is also why they are concerned about divorce, which is a family committing suicide.

In the most prophetic and most hated papal encyclical in history, *Humanae Vitae*, Pope Paul VI predicted that contraception would inevitably lead to abortion. The world laughed. But he has been proven right. Pro-choice propagandists constantly promote contraception as the *alternative* to abortion; and this seems reasonable, since contraception is first-line birth prevention while abortion is last-line birth prevention. Yet statistics consistently show that in almost all cases and in almost all places, increased contraception rates lead to more abortions, not fewer.

The next step is infanticide. For all the popular arguments that justify abortion also justify infanticide. It is only instinct and tradition that prevent it. And those are caving in rapidly, as shown by the world's reaction to the article in the *New York Times* in 1997 by Stephen Pinker, professor of psychology at MIT, who explicitly and candidly argued in favor of infanticide. As John Ellis noted, in the November 29, 1997, *Boston Globe*,

> His piece ran in the most prestigious newspaper in the world. His views on infanticide, apparently, are no longer considered out of the mainstream. For the reaction to Pinker's rationalization of infanticide was a deafening silence. A Lexus/Nexus search of commentary in the days and weeks following publication of Pinker's piece revealed "no matches" because no one, apparently, deemed it worthy of discussion. . . . Imagine for a minute that a distinguished MIT professor had written a piece for the *New York Times* Sunday magazine arguing that doctors who perform partial-birth abortions should be arrested on charges of second-degree murder. A majority of Americans believe partial-birth abortion is morally proximate to murder, and not without reason. Such an article, in the unlikely event of its publication, would have caused an uproar. The editors of the magazine would have been inundated with faxes, letters, e-mails, and phone calls. Subscriptions would have been canceled in protest. Newspaper columns would have been written expressing outrage and consternation. Liberal commentators would have scolded the *Times* for even allowing such "right-wing hate-mongering" to be included in its pages. But publish an article that advocates the decriminalization of infanticide and the media world yawns. . . . The right-to-life movement has long argued that once society adapts to the idea of aborting fetuses, it would

soon entertain the idea of killing infants. This argument used
to be thought specious, a non-sequitur, doom-saying of the
overworked imagination. Judging from Pinker's article and
the subsequent media reaction, it must now be regarded as
. . . true.

There is no morally significant difference between abortion
and infanticide, between killing a child a minute after birth
and killing a child a minute before birth. Or two minutes
before birth. Or three, or nine, or nine days, or nine weeks,
or nine months. But there is a *physically* significant difference
between killing a child one minute after birth, or nine minutes, or nine weeks, or nine months, on the one hand, and
nine *years* after birth, on the other hand. The difference is
that the nine-year-old can fight back. If fetuses were equipped
with little weapons to defend themselves against abortionists, the fight would be a little fairer and abortions a little
fewer.

Abortion destroys families in the most literal way: by literally ripping apart the most intimate and primordial family
unit of all, mother and baby. This is not rhetoric. This is
fact, painful fact—literally, physically painful fact. The rhetoric is found in its euphemistic coverups.

7. Sex

A seventh reason we fight against abortion is that we love
and respect and fight for sex.

This may sound strange if you have been reading the propaganda of *Cosmo* and *Playboy*; for they always paint abortion opponents as sexually repressed, joyless, imprisoned, and
unfree. Abortion is the sacrament of the Sexual Revolution.
Abortion, as last-ditch birth control, frees women to have

sex without babies and frees men even more from sexual responsibility.

We are pro-life to save sex from the Sexual Revolution, which is sex's greatest enemy, just as radical feminism is femininity's greatest enemy.

Sex is God's invention for originating life. Since we love the effect (human life), we love the cause—both the ultimate cause (God) and the proximate, instrumental cause (sex). It is because we love it that we resist its trashing. If you love your wife, you will not use her for a toy.

Of all fifteen points, this one will certainly have the hardest time winning a hearing. For our society is a society of sex addicts, and addicts simply cannot think clearly about their addiction, whether to cocaine, alcohol, sex, self-esteem, shopping, or autonomy.

I have been told repeatedly by pro-choice people, once our discussion becomes candid and heated, that the bottom line in the abortion battle is not about babies but about adult sex lives; that their one non-negotiable is that they will not let "us" tell "them" how to live; that they will practice their chosen sexual lifestyle come hell or high water or unplanned pregnancy.

Why should this surprise us? Of course abortion is about sex, for abortion is backup contraception, and contraception is the demand to have sex without babies. It is physically impossible for there to be an abortion without there having been sex; only sex makes the baby that abortion kills.

Abortion is the necessary trump card against the fearful "alternative lifestyle" of motherhood and family and responsibility, against the pre-sexual-revolution lifestyle. Abortion is the insurance against that fate worse than death which is called a family. Our no-fault insurance has removed our responsibility for car accidents, and no-fault divorce has removed our responsibility for marriage accidents; why should abortion not be our no-fault sexual insurance policy that removes our responsibility for sex accidents?

But what are these "sex accidents"? People! New little people, eternal souls created by God and destined for infinite and eternal happiness in Heaven. That's all.

How would you feel if you believed you were an accident? That means that the cause of your existence was not love, either human or divine. You were not loved into existence. You do not exist because of love. Love is not your first cause and therefore your meaning and final end. This is ultimately despair, the mind-set that leads to suicide, both social and individual.

The defenders of the Sexual Revolution usually accuse religious believers of having a negative view of sex while they have a positive one. Nothing could be more totally false. Let us just compare the two views.

Christians believe that sex is an image of trinitarian love. Catholics also believe that sex is one of the two greatest miracles in the world, the other being the Eucharist, for both are God's direct, miraculous doors by which he personally enters our world. In the Eucharist, he transforms bread and wine into the body and blood of his only begotten Son; in sex he transforms a sperm and an egg into a new person, a new "I", a new image of "I AM."

What is the alternative view of sex? That it is a biological accident that happens to offer a lot of transient recreational pleasure and passion. They say sex is a toy; we say it is a sacrament. So of course they say it is we who have the low, negative view and they who have the high, positive view. Right. No doubt they also say they have a high view of logic.

A philosophy of life that sees a pregnancy as a sexual accident is as insanely unnatural as one that sees nutrition as a gastronomic accident. We need to address one who believes such a philosophy with something more than argument—perhaps something more like exorcism. To save children's bodies from death we have to save adults' minds from insanity. Our pro-life rescue hospital has to include a psychiatric clinic.

And we certainly need to retool our society's "sex education", for most of it is exactly the opposite: unlearning rather than learning. It is unlearning the first and most obvious truism about sex that every human being in the history of the world knew as instinctively as he knew that mouths were for eating: that sex is for babies. Of course sex is for other things, too, besides babies, just as mouths are for other things, too, besides eating. But the fact that mouths are also for singing and talking and smiling does not mean that eating is an accident. Why should the fact that sex is for fun and love and intimacy mean that it is not for babies? But all those sex education programs seem to have worked remarkably well: we now no longer know what sex is for.

8. Violence

Our eighth reason for fighting abortion is to fight violence. Abortion is the most obvious, in-your-face example of violence. It is not just in your face, it *destroys* your face—and the rest of your body, too. Abortion is as violent as bombs or gas chambers, only smaller. Violence is unnatural, and life is natural.

What does that mean? Very simply, that if you let it alone, a human life grows from within as naturally and peacefully as a plant. But this understanding of nature is becoming increasingly incomprehensible to a generation raised on technological quick fixes and man-made "virtual realities". The very concept of "nature" as an intrinsic essence and principle of growth, and of a "natural" activity, is thought to be philosophically naïve or practically "repressive" today—because we want so much to justify unnatural acts, acts that do violence to nature: abortion, contraception, sodomy.

There is one very great advantage in abortion: giving an unwanted baby death instead of life, like all violence, is much quicker. Life takes time and patience. But our relationship to time is also radically changing: we try to "conquer" it as we try to "conquer" nature.

By the way, speaking of "unwanted babies" is misleading: there *are* no unwanted babies. There are babies who are unwanted by their biological parents, but there are thousands of adults waiting to adopt these babies. But the babies are hard to find because most of them are aborted. The situation is as absurdly grotesque as a poor farmer pleading with a rich farmer not to kill his extra cow, which he does not want, but to give it to the poor farmer—but he kills it anyway. Yes, it is insulting to compare a baby to a cow; is it any less insulting to call it an accident, or a lump of cells, or to make it a corpse?

We want to tell the world that violent solutions are not only wicked, but also lies. They do not even deliver the escape they promise. Each abortion attempts two murders, but it is harder to kill the mother's conscience than the baby's flesh, because the conscience is the heart of the soul, which is immortal. And the burden of guilt a mother carries around in her conscience after her abortion will be longer and heavier than the burden of the baby she carries in her body. Which brings us to our ninth reason:

9. Women

We fight abortion also because we fight for women. One of the biggest lies of abortionists is that they are "feminists". That is like calling cannibals "chefs". The most radical "feminists" are the most radically *anti*-feminine—like the legendary Amazons, who cut off one of their own breasts so that they could shoot a bow like a man. ("A-mazon" means literally "without a breast".) The Amazons destroyed their femininity so that they could imitate masculine violence, war, and killing—exactly like the so-called feminists today. Their name (Amazon) is apt, for in that breast is baby's milk, and behind that breast is a heart, and the pro-abortion feminist has dried up both of these icons of her femininity.

We provide alternatives to abortion not only to save babies but also to save women. To say "Please don't kill your baby" is also to say "Please don't kill your womanhood." That was the message of all the great early feminists, who saw abortion as the ultimate betrayal and abuse of women. Just as the French Revolution, which promised "liberty, fraternity, and equality", actually delivered instead totalitarian dictatorship, suspicious hate, and ruthless elitism, so the Sexual Revolution, which promised a liberation of femininity from male chauvinism and from oppressive stereotypes, has actually delivered instead the envy of masculine "autonomy" and the oppression of scalpels on babies' bodies and of propaganda on mothers' minds.

10. Children

We fight against abortion also because we fight for children. The point seems very obvious. But there is a Big Media Lie here: the stereotype of pro-lifers as hard-hearted, ignorant, dogmatic, intolerant Fascists and of pro-choicers as soft-hearted, enlightened, open, tolerant "liberals". What is "liberal" about forcing violent death on innocent babies? What is "tolerant" about killing? What is hard-hearted about wanting to save the holy innocents?

Appeal to compassion is a strong selling point today. Our culture may not respect many traditional values any more, but nearly everyone at least respects the value of compassion. So it is essential for the media propaganda machine to mouth the Big Lie very loudly here. And it is essential for us to infiltrate this machine and tell the simple truth. And if the media denies us our right to tell the truth, we must tell *that* truth about the media, so that the public can have compassion for *us* and, through us, for the children we have compassion for.

Pro-choice propagandists have very effectively driven a wedge between compassion for women and compassion for children. They want to rip apart the bodies of mothers and their children, so they first rip apart their interests. They set mother against child and child against mother. We should have no compassion on this lack of compassion. There may or may not be a "seamless garment" of pro-life issues in the public arena, such as the juxtaposition of abortion and capital punishment; but there is certainly a seamless garment of pro-baby and pro-mother compassion. It is more than a figurative "seamless garment"; it is a literal umbilical cord.

11. Survival

Another reason for fighting abortion is self-interest. As Dietrich Bonhoeffer wrote, "They came for the Jews, and I didn't speak up because I wasn't a Jew. Then they came for the Gypsies, and I didn't speak up because I wasn't a Gypsy. Then they came for the Communists, and I didn't speak up because I wasn't a Communist. Then, when they came for me, there was no one to speak up for me." Dostoyevsky wrote, "we are each responsible for all." John Donne wrote, "No man is an island . . . never send to know for whom the bell tolls; it tolls for thee."

The camel's nose is already under the tent, and the rest of the camel always follows the nose because it is a one-piece camel. The camel is "the culture of death". The nose is abortion. The rest of the camel includes infanticide, active euthanasia, assisted suicide, eugenics, genetic engineering, cloning, and harvesting fetal body parts in what Jeremy Rifkin calls *The Human Body Shop*; and finally, the replacement of "defective" or imperfect natural human beings with perfect, genetically engineered artificial human beings, à la *Brave New World*. This is (in C. S. Lewis' words) "the abolition of man". Your and my survival is at stake. Remember, it is a one-piece camel.

12. Religion

Abortion is indeed a religious issue, though not in the way our critics say. It is not just a Catholic issue or just a Christian one. It is a war between all religions and none. For all the religions of the world see life as a sacred mystery. Opposition to abortion is religious, but not sectarian. The idea that life is "sacred" is, by definition, a religious idea. But it does not belong to any one religion; it belongs to the human race. And its enemy is that tiny, powerful army of the arrogant who scorn the deepest convictions of ninety-nine out of every one hundred humans who have ever walked the earth as some silly, superstitious, stupid fallacy, fantasy, folly, or fear. If they abolish from our consciousness the very sense of the sacred, they can abolish the sense of the sacredness of lives; and if they abolish the sense of the sacredness of lives, they can abolish lives.

So the fight for the sanctity of life is literally a holy war because it is a war for holiness itself, a spiritual war to preserve the very idea of the spiritual.

13. Love of life

How much simpler could it be? We are pro-life because we love life. Even if some of us do not have religious beliefs, we love life and think it is a good thing for everyone, including "unwanted" babies. And we think it is a very bad thing to allow some humans—strong and large ones, with laws and weapons and medical know-how—to steal this good thing called life away from other humans simply because these others are weak and small and unprotected by laws, weapons, or knowledge.

How much simpler could it be?

14. Ethics

We are pro-life because we are pro-ethics, pro-justice. Abortion is simply wrong, unjust, unethical, unfair. It is not a complex issue. If it is not wrong for big, strong people to kill little, weak people just because they do not want them to live, then what could possibly be wrong? What could the word "wrong" possibly mean then? Only this (as one psychologist put it, seriously): "The only thing that's wrong is using the word 'wrong'." A most convenient philosophy for tyrants.

If there is any one moral rule that any morally sane person must admit, it is this one: Love people. Respect people. Treat people as ends, not means. Do not use them. That is Kant's "categorical imperative". Persons are ends, not means. Killing them certainly does not treat them as ends. It treats them as cockroaches.

Is it not amazing that many of the same people who deplore capital punishment against convicted murderers promote capital punishment against innocent babies? Apparently in their ethical system the crime of a baby being in a mother's way is deserving of death, but the crime of getting another adult out of your way by killing him is not.

15. The Image of God

I conclude with my final, and most non-negotiable, reason for fighting for life; the reason why we will never give up, why we can never give up. For we have no choice. We are not pro-choice. Here we stand. We cannot do otherwise. God help us.

For the face that confronts us is not just the tiny, innocent face of the human baby, whom we have procreated, but the enormous, innocent face of Almighty God, who has created us and the baby. It is his image that abortion kills. Abortion is homicide, and homicide is deicide because man is God's image, God's child. Abortion's victim is one of God's kids, and if you kill any good father's kids, you are far more his enemy than if you kill him. Do you think God is any less loyal to his kids than we are?

People often ask where God was in the Holocaust. The answer is that he was in the victims; he was gassed.

We all know that we will die. And we all instinctively know that when we die we will stop avoiding truth, because we will find truth unavoidable. If we believe in God we know why. We will stand before Truth, and Truth will say to us: "I was hungry, and you gave me no food. I was thirsty, and you gave me no drink. I was a stranger, and you did not welcome me; naked, and you did not clothe me; sick and in prison, and you did not visit me. I was in the womb, the place of life, and you slaughtered me." And we will ask, "Lord, when did we do this?" And he will answer: "Truly, truly I tell you: whatever you did to one of the least of these my brethren, you did to me."

Can any of us stand before those words? Can we even stand to risk hearing those words? Can we even bear to imagine hearing those words spoken to us?

There is an alternative: that when we die we will hear other words, both from the babies we helped to save and from the God who is their Father: "I was hungry and you gave me food. I was in danger and you rescued me. For whatever you did to one of the least of these, you did to me."

That is why we can never stop. We fight for the image of God.

What does the image of God look like today? Here are two answers, from the two sides in this war. One answer is the image of a man who loved God and his children so much, and who loved love so much, that he was crucified by those who hated love and loved hate. The Cross is an image of what happens when love meets hate, when good meets evil, when life meets death.

It is a familiar image, a beloved picture. Perhaps our society still believes in that picture. Or perhaps it is moving to another one. Here is its alternative. It looks very much like the old one, for it too contains a cross. But look where it is. It is in a work of "art" subsidized by the American government, created by Andres Serrano. He submerged a cheap plastic crucifix into a tube of his own urine and called it *Piss Christ*. It was exhibited across the country and paid for by your tax money.

Nothing but a few words of protest resulted. No one was punished, no laws were changed, no money changed hands, no one was fired at any government agency, and equally insulting works of "art" followed, including a picture of the Blessed Virgin Mary pelted with gobs of elephant dung and surrounded by photos of whores. What do you think would have been done if this occurred in any Muslim country and

it had been Muhammad who was insulted? Even Jesus could
never be dishonored like this in any Muslim country. Nor
could Mary.

Imagine a convicted murderer saved from the electric chair
by the love of the prison chaplain who chose to go to the
electric chair in his place. Now imagine this freed murderer
showing his gratitude to the chaplain who saved him by uri-
nating on the chaplain as he sat in the electric chair. That is
exactly what Mr. Serrano's work of "art" means.

We will never give up because we fight for God and for
man, his immortal image. We will fight for eternity because
we fight for eternity.

III

What Happens When an Irresistible Force Meets an Immovable Object?

A typical pro-life/pro-choice dialogue,
which addresses the fifteen most common pro-choice arguments

Note:
The two characters in this dialogue are taken from my forthcoming novel and have already appeared in print in another dialogue, *A Refutation of Moral Relativism* (Ignatius Press, 1999). Libby, the pro-choicer, is a "sassy, classy Black feminist", and 'Isa, the pro-lifer, is a "Muslim fundamentalist philosopher". Both are short-tempered, sharp-tongued, and direct.—P.K.

Some tedious preliminary prattle

Libby: I hate this.

'Isa: You hate what?

L: Where we are and what we have to do. We're not real, we're only characters in Professor Kreeft's book. And he's forcing us to do the impossible: to have a dialogue on abortion.

I: I disagree with all four things you said.

L: Of course you do. I didn't even know I said four things.

I: Of course you didn't.

L: OK, I'll bite. What four things?

I: First, that we're not real.

L: Of course we're not real. We're only characters in a book.

I: But the conclusion does not follow. In fact, just the opposite: We're real because we are characters in this book. Our author made us real. Do you think our author is writing this book about dreams? Ask the author whether we're real people or not. He has the authority to answer it, the author's rights.

L: Metaphysical subtleties! Who cares?

I: And your second mistake is that you said we were forced, not free.

L: So?

I: Do you think our author is writing this book about robots?

L: OK, OK, the same metaphysical subtlety.

I: Third—

L: This is getting tedious already.

I: Is it the numbers that bother you?

L: No, it's the numberer.

I: Third, you said we have to do the impossible. But we're doing it. We're having a dialogue.

L: You call this a dialogue? And even if it is, it's not on abortion.

I: It wasn't until you said the A-word. But it is now.

*Can we
dialogue
about
abortion?*

L: You really think a pro-choicer like me and a pro-lifer like you can have a rational dialogue on abortion?

I: Sure.

L: You probably also think the Red Sox can win a World Series, don't you? Or that computers can talk ordinary language. Or that you can find packages with the same number of hot dogs and hot dog rolls in the supermarket.

I: Why do you think we can't have a dialogue on abortion?

L: Because in my experience it never happens. Pro-lifers always use words as weapons to condemn pro-choicers, instead of listening and learning. And I suppose pro-choicers do, too, most of the time.

I: As a pro-choicer, are you bragging or complaining?

L: Complaining. Confessing, even.

I: Then why not repent and stop?

L: When you stop shooting at me, I'll stop shooting back at you.

I: Maybe that can happen.

L: Not with you. I know you. You're argument personified.

I: I'm not offering to forego argument. I'm offering to stop shooting at *you*.

L: No warm-fuzzy group-grope feel-good love-in for you, right?

I : Right! I'm not a feel-good addict, I'm a truth addict.

L: Yeah, right. Don't give me that line, 'Isa. I know you too well from all our other so-called dialogues. You're not addicted to truth, you're addicted to preaching and put-downs.

I: Well, believe it or not, today I want to listen and learn. In fact, I hope you do most of the talking. Because, believe it or not, I hope you can convince me I'm wrong, and that we should all just live and let live and be "pro-choice". Because if I believed that, it would save me a lot of sweat and trouble.

L: I'd love to believe you mean it. But your actions speak louder than words. You've always been an agitator and confrontational. I guess it's a guy thing.

I: No, if I were a woman I'd be just as confrontational about this topic. Especially if I were a mother. Do you know how confrontational animal mothers are when their children are threatened?

L: OK, so you're a hawk and I'm a dove. You're a war-monger and I'm a pacifist. That's just the way we are.

I: No, it's not just personal, it's principle. I don't see how there can be any other option than war when innocent children are threatened. How can I be a pacifist without compromising my principles?

L: Let me test you. Let's see whether you really want to listen and learn. Let me offer you something: a principled pacifism.

Pro-choice argument no. 1: Human fallibility

I: Based on what principle?

L: The principle of human fallibility. You pro-lifers are always so damned dogmatic. Suppose you begin instead with the premise that humans are fallible. Do you deny that principle?

I: No.

L: Then let's add a second one: your own humanity. (Though from our past experience, I'd say that's somewhat questionable.) Do you claim you are a human being?

I: This may be a shock to you, Libby, so perhaps you'd better sit down before I tell you. The answer is, Yes.

L: I think you know what a syllogism is, am I right?

I: Yes.

L: All humans are fallible, and 'Isa is a human, therefore 'Isa is fallible. Is there a fallacy there?

I: No.

L: So you get my point. It's a fact, it's not theory but data, that serious and intelligent and honest people of goodwill can and do take opposite positions, principled positions, on abortion. You don't have to demonize your opponents to disagree with them on a controversial issue like this.

Is abortion a clear evil?

I: I don't demonize pro-choicers. I don't even demonize abortionists. But I demonize abortion. Because I don't agree with you that it's a controversial issue at all. I say it is a very clear-cut evil.

L: But your position is in fact controverted. Most Americans don't agree with it. So it *is* controversial. You've got your head in the clouds of principles instead of along the ground of real people's attitudes.

I: Attitudes? Attitudes don't make morality.

L: I didn't say they did . . .

I: And you can't turn something clear into something controversial just by controverting it. If someone says that $2 + 2$ is 5, does that make "$2 + 2 = 4$" a controversial issue?

L: Of course not. But look at what you've done: you've assumed that abortion is like $2+4=4$.

I: Yes, I have. It's as clear, or almost as clear, that abortion is wrong as that $2 + 4 = 4$. If abortion's not wrong, nothing is wrong.

L: Now that's what I just can't have any sympathy for. I try to generate some sympathy for everyone I disagree with (that's my job, you know; I'm a psychological social worker), and frankly you're a real hard case. And I think you're typical of pro-lifers. You're so arrogant, so self-assured.

I: Who's being judgmental now?

L: You are! I'm only judging your judgmentalism. I'm only intolerant of your intolerance.

I: Have you ever heard of the law of non-contradiction?

L: Look, let's cut the cute rhetoric and get serious.

I: I didn't know the law of non-contradiction was "cute rhetoric". But I'm willing to get serious. How?

L: Do you really think we pro-choicers are clearly evil?

I: No, but I think you're clearly wrong. I judge your ideas, not you.

L: Then why do pro-choice people who aren't terribly wicked believe such wicked pro-choice ideas, according to you?

I: That's a good argument. I guess my answer is—

L: No, wait. I don't want to argue, I want to understand. So I want to understand you, and how you understand us, or misunderstand us. I want to listen. So please be honest and tell me exactly what you think and feel, instead of trying to win the argument.

I: OK. Here's my totally honest answer. I think a few of you *are* wicked. I think a lot more of you are very confused or very ignorant. And I think most of you are very sheepish and weak conformists who believe the pro-abortion propaganda of the mind-molders who have brainwashed you in the schools and in the media. I think you've been raped—in your minds, not your bodies. You're victims; that's why you will victimize babies.

Pro-life beliefs about pro-choice motives

L: And I'll bet you think that what you just said is really being polite to us, more polite than we deserve.

I: To be totally honest, yes. That's why I want to listen and learn, too, to learn something about you that I just can't understand. I don't understand how abortion—how brutally murdering her own unborn sons and daughters in her own womb—could be approved by any human being who still has her sanity, her moral common sense, and her instincts intact—especially a mother.

L: They're not mothers! They've chosen not to be mothers. Do you say that choice is always evil? That any woman who isn't a mother is a wicked woman?

I: But they *are* mothers. That's why abortion is wrong: not because they made the wrong choice to get pregnant—

maybe some did and maybe not—but because they're making the wrong choice now: to kill their own children that they've already conceived. I don't understand how a woman can believe that's not a terrible act, a terribly wicked act.

L: If you really want to understand, I'll try to tell you. But I don't want to get into another philosophical debate about it. You're the philosopher, I'm the psychologist. Debate is your thing, but dialogue is my thing.

I: I'll try to do your thing, because I really do want to learn what's in your head. And I'll believe you really want to learn what's in mine, as you said. But I can't guarantee you that I won't argue, because that's *part* of what's in my head: my reasons, my arguments.

L: I understand that as a philosopher you look at reasons. But you have to understand that as a psychologist I look at motives.

I: I understand that. But that's why you can't ignore my reasons, because my reasons *are* my motives. But . . . please let's not get into this kind of argument today. I really want to learn something new, not just win the argument: I really want to get inside your head. I really want to know how you, an apparently sane and moral person, can justify murdering your own children. Why doesn't that look like a clear and obvious evil to you, as it does to me?

L: Because you're assuming all sorts of things with that judgment. You're looking at only one thing, with tunnel vision. There are dozens of arguments, and dozens of other factors and aspects and points of view and real and deep disagreements about all of them. You're ignoring nine-tenths of the evidence: women's experience and women's

rights, changing social structures and needs and expecta-
tions, and the right to privacy and freedom and pluralism,
and the relation between civil law and morality—

Pro-choice
argument
no. 2:
There are
dozens of
arguments
and factors,
not just
one.

I: Wait—let me ask you something. Would you bring all
those other things in to justify slavery? Or lynching? Or
genocide? Or rape? Wouldn't you have the same simplistic "tunnel vision" about those things that I have about
abortion?

L: I knew you'd degenerate into arguing instead of
listening.

I: No, no, this *is* listening. I really want to know what
you think about those other things.

L: All right, then I'll tell you. I think those things are
very different from abortion. They're all clearly wrong, as
abortion is not. Nobody defends them, but half the people in America defend abortion.

I: So you think a thing is wrong only when everyone
says so? And a thing isn't wrong when half the people in
America defend it?

L: No, I don't think that. I don't think right and wrong
are nothing but creations of opinion polls, if that's what
you're thinking.

I: Then why . . .

L: Because the victim of a rape, or genocide, or lynching
is obviously one of us.

I: "Us"? You mean adults? Big people? Smart people?
Who do you mean by "us"?

L: People, of course.

I: Oh. So it all comes down to whether the victim of abortion is a person or not, then.

L: No, it doesn't *all* come down to that. That's not the only question. The other elements have to be factored in, too.

I: Maybe that's where we differ. I don't think they do.

L: I think that *is* where we differ. I don't have that simplistic tunnel vision of yours. I think about the fetus, but I also think about a hundred other things, especially the mother. Why don't you?

I: I do think about them. But I don't think even a million other things can make it right to kill your own children. I don't think anything can.

"Fetuses" or "fetal humans"? **L:** But your very language begs the question. You call them "children", not "fetuses".

I: No, I call them both children and fetuses. They're fetal children, fetal humans, fetal persons. A "fetus" isn't another species. A fetal ape isn't a worm, it's an ape at the fetal stage of development. And a fetal human isn't an ape, it's a human at the fetal stage of development. It's *you* at one stage of your development. Once you were a zygote, then an embryo, then a fetus, then an infant, then a youth. then a teenager, then an adult. "Adult" isn't a noun, it's an adjective: adult *human being*. The same with "infant"—it means "infant *human being*." So with "fetus". That's what the word *means*: fetal *human*.

L: So you think you can solve the problem just by arbitrarily choosing to use words in your way instead of my way?

I: No, I think that's what *you're* doing. Neither of us can solve a problem just by changing the language.

L: Well, then we need to have neutral language if we're going to have an open dialogue.

I: So what do you propose to call abortion? "The final solution to the pregnancy problem"?

L: See? That's why I hate talking to you! You said you'd put your guns away, and then you shoot from the hip.

I: I'm sorry. I'll try to button my lip. But it's hard to talk about an atrocity in clinical terms. It's unnatural. I know— "atrocity" isn't neutral language either. I'll try to neuter myself.

L: How can I believe you're sincere? Even your repentance is sarcastic.

I: And you, on the other hand, are never sarcastic with me. Right.

L: Look, let's at least make one desperate try to explain ourselves to each other without any sarcastic or put-down words, in neutral language that doesn't beg the question.

I: I'm game.

L: So will you listen with an open mind now to what I feel about all those issues you dismissed a minute ago?

I: You mean women's rights and privacy, and all that?

L: "All that", yes.

I: If you want me to be perfectly honest with you, I'll have to say No.

L: What?!

I: I won't—rather, I *can't* listen to anything you say about those issues with an open mind. Not yet—not until you convince me that it won't be a total waste of time, that it could possibly make any difference what you say. Because—

L: Because you want to stick your head in the sand and ignore all the other issues about abortion and only think about the fetus.

I: I'm not ignoring those issues, I'm prioritizing them. I mean *de*-prioritizing them. Because they're all relative to the issue of whether the fetus is an innocent human being.

L: Why do you insist on seeing it that way?

I: Because if the fetus *is* an innocent human being, then killing it can't be justified for any reason. Nothing can excuse deliberate murder. So let's not waste time with looking at the excuses. We both know what I'm going to say about them. I don't think "the end justifies the means", even a very good end, if the means is wicked. I hope you agree. I wouldn't commit a murder for *any* reason, and I hope you wouldn't either. Would you?

If abortion is murder, can anything justify it?

L: No, not murder.

I: So the one thing that divides us is whether abortion is murder. I understand how you can justify it if you think it's not murder, and you must understand how I condemn it if I think it *is* murder, so we both understand each other there, we understand each other's principle, I think. What I don't understand is why you think abortion isn't murder, and what you don't understand is why I think it is.

L: What I don't understand is why *you* don't understand that not everyone sees it your way.

I: I understand *that* they don't, but I don't understand *why* they don't. That's what I'm trying to find out from you in this dialogue.

L: You don't understand why everyone in the world doesn't see it your way! Wow. That's a confession. We should all see it your way, right?

I: Of course! But not because it's my way, but because it's true.

L: Wow! I can't believe what I'm hearing. I think I *am* coming to understand you better: "My way" equals "true", right? Is that your principle?

I: No, no, it's not true because I believe it; I believe it because it's true. Look, it's simple logic: If the fetus is a human being, then abortion is murder. How much simpler could it be?

L: So that means that women have no rights over their bodies, and no right to privacy, and . . . and . . .

I: Of course women have rights over their own bodies, but the fetus is somebody else's body. And sure, there may be a right to privacy, but when one person kills another, that's not privacy. You're in private when you're alone, but you can't murder another when you're alone, when there's no other there. Murder is a *public* act.

L: You're arguing now instead of dialoguing.

I: No, I'm trying to explain to you why I think it's such a simple issue. All the other issues are relative to this one: *If* the thing abortion kills is not a thing but a person, a human being, then abortion is murder. And if it is, then no argument can justify it, no excuse can excuse it, no other issue can trump it.

L: And if it's not, then no argument can justify forcing a woman to carry a baby for nine months and give birth against her will, forcing her by laws and threats *never* to have an abortion.

I: I agree with you! Nothing less than another human life has rights over her life.

L: Oh. That's encouraging. You do really understand that much of me, anyway.

I: Yes. And do you really understand this much of me: that *if* the fetus *is* a human being, it's never right to kill it?

L: I guess so. Yes, I'd say that's a reasonable principle: "Thou shalt not kill." You're a pacifist, then?

I: No, I'm not.

L: So you don't agree totally with the Ten Commandments?

I: I do. But the Commandment doesn't actually say "Thou shalt not kill" in Hebrew; it says "Thou shalt not *murder*." Killing the guilty is not necessarily forbidden, only killing the innocent. Murder is killing *innocent* persons.

L: So you're not a pacifist. You're in favor of killing sometimes. When? What about capital punishment?

I: That's a red herring. It doesn't change whether abortion is right or wrong. Some pro-lifers *are* pacifists, and most are against capital punishment, but you don't have to agree with those two positions to be against abortion.

L: I think I understand you a little better now, at least.

I: But I still don't understand you. How do you justify abortion? What do you do with the simple, obvious pro-life argument?

L: I thought we were dialoguing, not arguing.

I: We're trying to understand each other. And I want to understand what goes on in your head when you hear the fundamental pro-life claim.

L: Which is ... ?

The most basic pro-life argument

I: That deliberately killing innocent people is murder, and abortion deliberately kills innocent people, therefore abortion is murder.

L: Do you want me to refute your syllogism or share my feelings?

I: Refute my syllogism, please! Your feelings don't go any farther than your skin, but your refutation, if you have one, goes around the world. It goes to every abortion and every pro-lifer in the world. And if it's true, it goes to me, too. And I'll repent and convert and switch and work for your side from now on, if only you can show me that it's true.

L: So we have to do logic.

I: We all have to do logic, all the time, whenever we think, just as we all have to breathe air all the time whenever we breathe.

L: So you demand that I do logic.

I: *I* don't demand it; honesty demands it.

L: I guess I have to answer your argument.

I: If you can.

L: Of course I can.

I: How? There are only three ways, you know: finding an ambiguous term, or a false premise, or a logical fallacy.

L: You don't have to give me a lesson in logic.

I: Good. But if I don't have to give you a lesson in logic, then you have to give me one of those three things. Which will it be?

L: That's easy: an ambiguous term: "human being". You say abortion is murder because the fetus is a human being. But I say it's only a human *life*. Of course it's biologically human, not an ape. But it's not yet a human person. We all make that distinction. Every cell in your body has human life, genetically distinctive human life. You could clone another human being from any one of your cells. But that one cell is not another individual person.

Pro-choice argument no. 3: Distinguish "human life" from "human person"

I: So what makes a human person? What is a human being?

L: A biologically whole individual of the human species.

I: And a human fetus isn't that?

L: No. Certainly, a zygote isn't. At that moment, at the moment it's first conceived, it's just one cell. How could you say that's a whole human being? *Do* you really believe it is?

I: Yes.

L: Then what's *your* definition of a human being?

I: Exactly the same as yours: a biologically whole individual of the human species. Even a human zygote is that.

Is a zygote a human person?

It's not just one more cell in the mother's body. It's a new body, in its most primitive stage.

L: So you really believe that one cell is a complete human being.

I: Yes. It's not completely *grown*, but it's completely *human*.

L: So is each cell in your body.

I: But the zygote is completely *individual*, it's completely *different*. It's got its own genetic code. If you cloned any cell in the mother's body, you'd get a replica of Mommy. But if you cloned the zygote, you'd get a totally different person.

L: So that microscopic thing is a human being.

I: Yes. "A person's a person, no matter how small." Or didn't you read Dr. Seuss when you were a kid?

L: I find that totally ridiculous.

Feelings vs. facts

I: That tells us something about your subjective feelings, but it doesn't tell us anything about objective facts.

L: The mother's feelings are facts, too. A mother who gets an abortion doesn't feel she's murdering a person.

I: Sometimes she does. Why else does she feel so guilty about it?

L: Because you pro-lifers have aborted her self-esteem with your guilt trip, that's why!

I: And you say she has no real reason to feel guilty, right?

L: Right.

I: Then we need to find out whether she has or hasn't. And if the fetus is a human being, she has. And if it isn't, she hasn't. So it all depends on what the fetus is.

L: So the mother's feelings just don't count for you, is that it?

I: No . . .

L: Then let's look at them, and not just at the fetus.

I: But we already know the mother's feelings; we need to find out what a fetus is, whether it's a human being or not.

L: You like to separate those two things totally, don't you?

I: To *distinguish* them, yes. Because what makes a fetus human or not is fetal facts, not fetal feelings.

L: You're big on logic, I know.

I: No, it's not just for logical reasons, but for moral reasons, for human reasons. It's terribly important practically. You should know that. Your own people suffered from the same "logical" mistake! Suppose you were living in 1860, or whenever the Supreme Court came out with *Dred Scott*. You'd be declared less than human, you'd be defined as the property of a person rather than a human person, just because nine white judges felt that way about you. Would that make you property? Would that make you not a person?

L: I don't accept that analogy. That's a false analogy. And it's very insulting to me. And I'll bet you haven't the faintest idea why, do you?

I: No, I don't.

L: And you don't even care much about my feelings, do you?

I: Not as much as I care about your reasons. Because they're what justify your behavior.

L: No, they're what justify *your* behavior maybe, philosopher.

I: Look, are you saying that abortion is OK, and a fetus isn't a person, because the mother feels OK about it and because you feel not-OK about my analogy?

"Arguing" vs. "under- standing"?

L: I'm saying that we've descended into argument. We were supposed to be learning from each other, under- standing each other.

I: I don't see how we can understand each other if we don't understand each other's reasons.

L: I gave you my reason: Abortion is OK because a fetus isn't a person.

I: So it's got human *life*, but it's not a human *person*.

L: Right.

I: Is it a human *being*?

L: Word games! Look what you're doing: you're assum- ing that what it is *doesn't* depend on how I feel about it emotionally, but that it *does* depend on how you define it logically. What's sauce for the goose is sauce for the gan- der, 'Isa!

I: You're absolutely right. I'm very glad to hear you say that. So it doesn't depend on anybody else's feelings *or* definitions. It depends on what it is in itself. Our definitions of it can be right or wrong, then, and our feelings about it can be right or wrong, too.

L: Of course.

I: So let's look at what it is.

L: All right, let's. Let's look at this thing you call a person. It has no brain, no nervous system, no organs of any kind at all. It can't do a single one of all the things everyone calls human. It can't think, or feel, or choose, or see, or love, or play the sax, or surf.

Pro-choice argument no. 4: Zygotes can't do anything personal

I: If I find one thing it can do, and does, that only a human person can do, would that convince you it's a human person?

L: I guess so. If it quacks like a duck and looks like a duck and lays duck eggs like a duck, it's a duck.

I: But it *can* do one thing only a human person can do.

L: The zygote? What? It can't do *anything* yet.

I: It can grow into you.

L: Oh. But so can any one of your cells, by cloning. But killing one cell isn't murder. So killing a zygote isn't murder, either. There's no difference in principle.

I: There's a big difference in principle: one cell from an adult's body doesn't grow into you; you have to clone it, artificially. But the zygote does grow into you, naturally, by its own nature. So the zygote has a different nature from one cell of an adult.

L: It's got human nature, and so does every cell in my body. What do you mean, "a different nature"?

I: I mean it's a unique individual person, not just a part of a person.

L: It's a human life, I admit, but that doesn't make it a human person.

I: So it's a human *life*, and a human *being*, but not a human *person*.

L: Right. And only persons have rights, including a right to life. Do you deny that?

I: No. But I believe all human beings are persons. Do you think there's another kind of human being that isn't a person? Whom do you put in that class besides the unborn? And why aren't they persons? The handicapped, maybe? The mentally handicapped? Pro-lifers?

L: I think I'm having second thoughts about one pro-lifer.

I: Stop playing cute and answer the question, Libby!

L: Stop playing God and telling me what to do, 'Isa!

I: I'm not playing God. I'm playing "equal human being". I'm playing by the Golden Rule. I'll be very glad to answer all your questions. Won't you answer mine?

L: Of course I will. And will you answer mine?

I: Yes. Which one?

What makes a person?

L: What do *you* say makes a person'? Is it self-consciousness, or choice, or love, or empathy, or what? Which is the personal act, the act that defines a person?

Because that's going to be what gives it rights, including the right to life.

I: They're *all* personal acts.

L: And the fetus can't do any of them. So it's not a person.

I: No, because it's not any one act on the list, but the relation of the personal acts to the actor that makes for a person.

L: What do you mean by that?

I: Let me put it in the form of a choice, a multiple choice test. Which do you choose? Possibility Number One: a person is one who is *presently performing* some of these personal acts. If you choose that answer, then sleeping persons stop being persons when they sleep. So they don't have rights then, and it's OK to kill them. You don't want to say that. Possibility Number Two: a person is one with *a present capacity* to perform personal acts. That would include sleepers as persons, but not people in a coma. You don't want to say it's OK to kill them, so Possibility Number Two won't work either. Possibility Number Three is that a person is someone with *a past history* of performing personal acts. But that would mean that a twenty year old who was born in a coma twenty years ago and is going to come out of it in two minutes is not a person, and it would be OK to kill him as long as you did it before he came out of his coma. You don't want to say that. Also, if you choose Possibility Number Three, there can't ever be a first personal act, a personal act without a past history of personal acts. That would mean that it's logically impossible to have any person at all, ever, by that definition. So let's try Possibility Number Four: a person is someone with *a present capacity* for performing *future* personal acts. But that would mean that dying persons aren't persons and that there can't be any last personal act, and that's just as logically impossible as Possibility Number Three, which made it impossible for there ever to be any first personal act. So the only answer left, I think, is Possibility Five, which is what common sense has always used to define a person: a person is someone with *an inherent capacity, a natural capacity* for performing personal acts, given the right conditions, including time and growth. A person is someone with a certain nature, a certain essence, that by nature can perform personal acts like thinking and loving.

L: I see why you set it up that way: so that the one-celled zygote could be a person too. That's the pro-life definition of a person. Of course. You tailor your definition to your assumption about abortion.

I: No, you've got me backwards. I didn't begin with the premise that zygotes are persons and then fit my definition of a person to that premise. I began with the commonsense definition of a person, with everybody's definition—everybody except pro-choicers. But if you have your own definition, let's hear it. If it's not Number Five, is it One, or Two, or Three, or Four? Or do you have a Number Six?

L: We don't need a definition of a person to know that a microscopic single cell isn't a person.

I: Now who's tailoring her definition to her assumption about abortion?

L: Do you really believe that most people think a zygote is a person?

I: If they know enough science, yes. Because you were once a zygote. Every person was.

L: That's only a potential person. It's not a thinker, or lover, or chooser; it's only a potential thinker, or chooser, or lover, or whatever.

Pro-choice argument no. 5: Only a potential person?

I: But what is it actually? There's got to be something actually there, in the human zygote, that accounts for the fact that it's got a potentiality that is not in the zygote of any other animal. If that something wasn't already there, it could never become a thinker, or lover, or whatever. And that something is in its nature, its essence, from its very beginning; it's not added to it later, from outside. It unfolds from within. Like a baby being born. That tiny thing is already a fully programmed individual human being. Everything from sex to eye color to a taste for olives is already there. And if those accidental qualities are already there, the essence must be too. A person's a person, no matter how small.

L: It doesn't have a brain at all. It doesn't have any organs at all. How can it be a person? That's just not logical.

I: Just the opposite. *You have to be a human being to grow a human brain.* From the very first step. What's not logical is that something that's *not* a human being can grow a human brain from within.

L: Sure, it will have a brain, and it will think, and it will be a human person. But it's not doing anything yet.

I: Yes it is: it's growing a human brain and the rest of a human body.

L: So what is it, if it's not a human body?

I: It is a human body. What else could it be? It's human, and it's a body.

L: So you feel that killing it is murder.

I: No, I don't *feel* it. I *think* it, I *believe* it. We obviously don't *feel* the kind of bond with an embryo that we feel with a fully formed born baby.

L: And you want just to discount feeling altogether, Mister Philosopher?

I: No. I recognized the fact that most people let their feelings move them more than their thought. That's why I think women who have abortions aren't as wicked as Nazis who murder Jews or whites who lynch Blacks. And that's why most people feel ambivalent about abortion.

L: Oh, so you do understand that much, at least. Congratulations.

I: But how we feel about a thing can't be the standard for what the thing is and what rights it has, and whether it has a right to life. Most people don't feel the same kind of bond with deformed babies that they do with perfect babies, either; does that mean deformed babies aren't human?

L: No . . .

The relation between abortion and infanticide

I: You don't believe infanticide is OK, do you?

L: Of course not.

I: Why not? What justifies abortion that doesn't also justify infanticide? What makes infanticide wrong that doesn't make abortion wrong, too?

L: I guess I'll have to think about that one. Maybe I'll be forced to justify some infanticide, too.

I: I'm sorry I asked the question! Sometimes good logic can force you to do to bad things, just to be logically consistent.

L: I need to take a break for a minute. There's coffee over here. Let's give our tired brains a rest for a minute and come back and finish later, OK?

I: OK.

---

*Defining a
"person"*

L: Before the coffee, you pretty much tore up my definition of a person. Let's see whether I can return the favor. What's *your* definition of a person?

I: One who has a natural capacity to perform personal acts like thinking and choosing.

L: But she can do that only if there's a second factor present: she's old enough and developed enough.

I: That's true, And there's a third factor that has to be present, too: the physical circumstances that allow it: she's not drugged or chained or brain damaged.

L: Right.

I: But the circumstances allow the personal acts to happen only if there's a person there in the first place. They're like a catalyst for a chemical reaction. No set of circumstances could let a cat perform personal acts like thinking and choosing.

L: That's true. So what?

I: So factor three, the circumstances, presupposes factor one, the nature of a person. But so does factor two, the degree of development. You can be developed enough to think or choose only if you're a person in the first place. A mature cat can't think rationally any more than a kitten can.

L: That's obvious. What's your point?

I: The point is that your acts follow your being, your essence, your nature. You can't have personal acts unless you are a person. But you could be a person without being able to perform personal acts, whether because you're prevented by external circumstances like drugs or because you're not developed enough yet. A two-day-old infant can't choose or talk yet either, but he's a human being.

L: But there's a much bigger difference between the infant and the zygote than between the infant and the adult.

I: But both are only a difference in degree. And that can't make it right to kill. There's a bigger difference between the teenager and the infant than between the teenager and the young adult; does that mean it's OK to kill infants?

Difference in degree or in kind? **L:** Maybe it's all a difference in degree and not a difference in kind at all, so that when there's more of all that personal stuff there, it's more wrong to terminate it, and when there's less there, it's less wrong.

I: You can't bring yourself to say "kill it", can you? OK, let's examine that possibility. A ten-year-old girl doesn't have her reproductive system fully developed yet, and she still doesn't have all her language skills and her education fully in place. So do you want to say that it's not quite as bad to kill a ten-year-old as it is to kill a forty-year-old?

L: No, of course not.

I: But you do say that it's not as bad to kill a zygote as to kill a fetus, and not as bad to kill a one-month-old fetus as to kill an eight-month-old fetus.

L: I think so. That feels right.

I: Are you thinking or feeling? I think your first choice has to be whether you use thinking or feeling to make your moral choices.

L: Feeling isn't just sentiment, you know. It's intuition. It sees things, too. "The heart has its reasons, which the reason does not know."

I: Oh, I know that. But the human heart can also be blind and wicked, can't it? The heart of a Nazi "sees" the inhumanity of the Jews just as we "see" their humanity. We have to *check* our hearts, judge our hearts.

L: By reason, which is higher than love for you, right?

I: No, I didn't say that. It's just that hearts are subjective and individual and different. But reason is objective, universal, and equal—it imposes the same standards for everyone. That's why we're arguing now: to check out by reason which set of feelings is right.

L: And look what you've done: we were supposed to share our feelings and we ended up arguing. You broke our rules.

I: And that's wrong—to break the rules that we both agreed to—right?

L: Yes.

I: See? You're using logical reasoning to criticize my act of breaking the rules; and that's exactly what I'm doing to criticize your act of abortion, or tolerating abortion. You can't avoid reasoning.

L: I'm not avoiding anything. I just want to tell you what I feel as well as what I think.

I: Fine. Then please tell me what you think about this: you say that only some human lives are persons, right?

L: Did I say that?

I: You said that fetuses have human life, but they're not yet persons, with a right to life.

L: OK then.

I: So even if you have human life, you still have to qualify to pass the test of personhood and right to life.

L: There's a line somewhere there, yes.

I: So only the achievers, only the successful, only those who function well enough, make it.

L: I didn't say that. I'd draw the line at birth. I recognize that other people draw the line at other places. I'm tolerant of that, unlike you. I'm pro-choice. I'm not dogmatic. I don't say there's only one line. You do. You want to impose your philosophy on everybody. I think you've got a "will to power" problem 'Isa.

The will to power

I: Let's see who's got the "will to power" problem. *Wherever* the line is drawn, whether at birth or at I.Q. or at brain capacity, *you draw the line.* You draw it where you will. So it's the will of the stronger, the will of the born adult, that draws the line that excludes the weaker, the unborn. That looks like "the will to power" to me.

L: So you label me with Nietzsche and the Nazis! I guess you have to label me a racist and a warmonger and an anti–Semite, too, right?

I: No, I'm not labeling you, I'm labeling your philosophy. And my label isn't "Nazi".

L: But it *is* "murderer".

I: Your philosophy, yes! It justifies murder. Look!—ask yourself this question, honestly: *Why* do you draw the line there, at birth? Isn't it the same reason the Nazis drew the line between Aryan and Jew? Because they wanted to kill them! Why did the whites who lynched Blacks draw the line at race? Because they wanted to kill them! Whomever you want to kill, you label sub-human, to justify the killing. That's rationalizing your will to power.

L: Oh, so now you're the great psychologist pontificating about my hidden motives!

Who draws the line between persons and nonpersons, and why?

I: What else is it? If you won't let nature draw the line, if your standard isn't the nature of the thing you're killing, then your standard is something artificial, not natural: the artificial man-made line that *you* draw. You do it: you draw that line. That's your choice, your deed, your responsibility. That's always been done, throughout history: whenever the people in power want to kill somebody, they re-draw the lines. The Ku Klux Klan and the Nazis didn't call fetuses sub-human, because they didn't want to kill fetuses. You don't call Blacks or Jews sub-human because you don't want to kill Blacks or Jews. But you want to kill fetuses, so you call them sub-human. It's the killers who determine the criteria for personhood.

L: So you're calling me a killer. What a great exercise in human understanding this conversation has become! I'm outa here. If that's the kind of chop you're going to give my head when I put it on your block, I'm not coming near it any more.

I: That's why you're giving up? Not because you have nothing more to say?

L: I've got plenty to say, but not to the meat cleaver.

I: Suppose I promised to be very nice?

L: I don't think you're capable of it. But do you really want to try?

I: Yes; do you?

L: (Pause.) OK, one more time, just out of curiosity. Perhaps the leopard *can* change his spots. Let me attack you for a change. You say you want to let nature define a human person. I say that's biologism.

Pro-choice argument no. 6: Against "biologism"

I: What's that?

L: Defining persons in a merely biological way. Membership in a biological species can't be what makes persons sacred, or whatever gives you a right to life.

I: Why not?

L: Because membership in a biological species is material, and being a person is spiritual. Membership in a biological species can't give you a right to life any more than membership in a race, a biological sub-species. If racism is wrong, so is species-ism.

I: I see. But I don't think I did define human beings in a merely biological way. I wouldn't do that, because I believe a human being is not a merely biological reality. In fact, my claim that all humans are persons is just the opposite of biologism: it's the claim that all humans have souls. That's what makes them sacred. Their bodies are sacred for the same reason churches and synagogues and mosques are: they're the temples of those souls.

L: I believe we have souls too, but how do you know a zygote has a soul?

Do zygotes have souls?

I: It's already growing a human brain and nervous system, so it must have a human soul to guide that growth.

L: And you claim to know that for sure? Did you get a letter from God about it? Do you see a label on the zygote saying: "Warning: Contents Contain One Soul"?

I: No. Frankly, I'm not absolutely certain that the zygote has a soul. But are you certain that it doesn't? I'm being totally frank with you; will you be totally frank with me? I don't know for sure. That's why I won't abort it: I don't *know* whether it's a fully human person. I *think* it is. Now will you tell me exactly what you think? Do you claim to know that it isn't a person, with a soul?

L: Well . . .

I: Careful now! Because if you do, then the shoe is on the other foot: when we began, you accused me of being arrogant and dogmatic and claiming to know too much, and *you* were the careful, skeptical, humble one.

L: No, I don't claim to know.

Which one is arrogant?

I: So you *don't* know that it's *not* a human being?

L: No.

I: Then why do you want to let it be killed? Isn't that pretty intolerant? Isn't that "imposing your values on others"? In fact, it's something much worse than "imposing values"; it's imposing death. It's murder.

L: Only assuming your belief, that it's a person.

I: But if you don't know that that belief is wrong, aren't you taking a terrible chance that you're tolerating the supremely intolerant act of murder? I don't call that "tolerant".

L: But you're just as intolerant on the mother who wants an abortion. If you want to compel her by law not to have an abortion, you're imposing your values on her by force.

I: Do you really think it's just as intolerant, and just as much a use of force, when we prevent one person from killing another, as it is when we kill a person? Is nine months of unwanted pregnancy as terrible a form of violence as sudden, bloody murder?

L: You're assuming the fetus is a person.

I: No, you're assuming it's not. I'm assuming only that we don't know.

Pro-choice argument no. 7: All is gradual

L: OK, let's go with that, then: we don't know. And that gives us a reasonable compromise between pro-choice and pro-life. It's all gradual, it's all relative, there's no black or white. There's no clear, absolute distinction between what is a person and what isn't. Surely that's the position that fits the scientific data. Everything grows gradually—every one of those characteristics that we listed that make a person: thinking, feeling, loving, choosing, relating to others. It doesn't emerge suddenly, like a jack-in-the-box. God doesn't look down on earth and when he sees that a body is ready, whenever that is, whether it's at conception or at birth or some time in between, he suddenly reaches up into Heaven and grabs a soul and sticks it into its body. It's you pro-lifers who love simplistic, black-or-white thinking like that. But reality is gray, not black or white. You're unrealistic.

I: So personhood develops gradually.

L: Yes. And here's a good reason for thinking so: what psychologists call the psycho-somatic unity. The soul and body aren't two things, like a ghost and a machine; they're two dimensions of one thing, like the meaning of a poem and the words of the poem. They both develop gradually. The only meaningful way to talk about the soul is to talk about the body, and everything there is gradual.

I: I thoroughly agree with you. That's why I'm pro-life.

L: Come again?

I: I agree: the body is our clue to the soul, and the body keeps developing gradually, with no sharp break anywhere—except one: at conception. That's where the body begins, so that's where the soul begins, too. That's where *you* began.

Do persons begin at birth?

L: Why not birth?

I: Because birth is a process, not a sudden act. But at conception, there's a radically new thing. Once, there was no me, then—presto! A tiny me, frantically growing and multiplying from the very first moment, just like the universe right after the Big Bang.

L: A one-celled person? Do you know how many cells you have now? Trillions!

I: Why not? Once, the universe was a one-thing universe. Now it's a trillion-thing universe.

L: Your analogy proves nothing.

I: But it illustrates a possibility. And it shows the difference between a relative difference and an absolute difference. The difference between one and a trillion is relative; the difference between zero and one is absolute. Once, you did not exist. Then, you exist. When did that happen? At your sweet sixteen party? At your birth? When you became "viable"? We all know when it happened: when your mother's egg and your father's sperm, each with its own identity and genetic code, stopped being themselves, died to their own identity, and together made a new thing, with its own genetic code, its own identity. If the body is our best clue to the soul, zygotes have souls, because they have genetically distinctive bodies from the beginning.

L: What I mean by "soul" is something I can relate to, something that can feel pain, and see me, and love me . . . The zygote doesn't do anything "soulish" until it develops organs.

I: What do you think makes your body grow? That's your soul, too, and it's working from the very beginning.

L: No, that's just my body.

I: Then what makes the difference between a dead body and a living body, if not the soul? No body parts leave the body at death. Not one cell, not one molecule, not one atom leaves a body at the point when it dies. The life-force leaves it. That's the soul.

L: If the soul is just the life-force, then animals have souls, too.

I: It's not *just* the life force, but that's one of its functions. And yes, animals have animal souls.

L: Then it's wrong to abort animals, too. And even plants, because they're alive, too.

I: No, because they don't have human souls, rational souls, personal souls.

L: OK, then, it's all right to kill a fetus when it's only got the animal soul, that makes its body grow, and it only becomes wrong to kill it when it has a human soul, that starts doing some human things, the things on our list.

I: But that means we get two or three souls: first a plant soul, then an animal soul, then a human, rational soul. Do you really think we have three souls? That we get one after the other, gradually, in the womb? And that we lose one after the other, gradually, at the other end of life, when we die? Or does one soul do all the work: growing, and sensing, and thinking?

L: No, it's one soul. Three souls is bad psychology.

I: Then the soul begins at conception, because that's when we begin to grow. We never have a body without a soul. You're right to make fun of that picture of God reaching into Heaven to grab a soul to stick it into a pre-existing body.

Do souls begin when bodies begin, at conception?

L: So you recognize one and only one sharp dividing line in human life: conception and nothing else?

I: Actually, there are two sharp dividing lines, not one: the beginning and the ending. Death is as absolute as conception. And that's what anyone who wants an abortion *does* recognize: that dividing line. You don't recognize the difference between the two persons, the mother and her baby—you don't grant personhood to the baby—but you do recognize the difference between a live baby and a dead one. If you want an abortion, you're not satisfied until the baby is dead.

L: What a horrible thing to say!

I: What a horrible thing to do!

L: What you said is terribly cruel and insensitive.

I: Perhaps so. But it's true. If it isn't, tell me why it isn't. "If you want an abortion, you're not satisfied until the baby is dead"—of course that's true. If it weren't, if you *were* satisfied with the baby alive, you wouldn't be in an abortion clinic!

L: She doesn't want a dead baby, she wants a free woman.

I: And is the baby's death just "collateral damage", like civilians killed by a bomb in wartime? The baby is not the target?

L: I knew we couldn't do this. We began with dialogue, then we regressed into argument, and now we've descended into rhetoric.

I: Rhetoric? Rhetoric? What could be more simple and literal than what I just said? Where's the rhetoric?

L: This always happens with you pro-lifers.

I: Reality check, you mean? Facts, you mean? I plead guilty.

L: Can we give up now, or do we have to keep up this charade just because our author is on your side?

I: We have to keep up the argument. You know that. But not just because our author wants to. But because we have to be honest. We have to look at facts and give reasons. Reasons for killing or not killing—isn't that an important enough issue to have good reasons for? We're trying to draw a line, a reasonable line, between what it's all right to kill and what it's not all right to kill. And I still haven't heard a single reason for any other line except conception.

Pro-choice argument no. 8: Viability is the dividing line

L: Viability.

I: No, viability won't work because that varies with accidental things and external things like place. A five-month-old fetus that's viable in modern America, with incubators, isn't viable in Borneo, or a hundred years ago. It's very simple: there's something there in that womb; maybe it's a person and maybe not, but whatever it is, how can what it really is depend on what machines happen to exist out there in the outside world? Does a preemie suddenly become a person when an incubator arrives?

L: No. There's no sudden line. It's all gradual.

I: Then it's not as bad to kill a ten year old as a twenty year old? I thought we went through that already.

L: Birth is the legal dividing line.

I: But is the law good? Is it moral? Is it reasonable? That's what we're arguing about. We all know what the law is. We don't need to argue about that. I'm saying it's unreasonable and immoral for the law to say you can kill a baby one minute before birth but not one minute after birth. And if it's not right one minute before birth, it's not right two minutes before birth either, or three, or four, or four thousand, or any time at all! As soon as there's somebody there, it's wrong to kill. How could the Supreme Court judges miss that simple point?

L: They said we don't know when this "something" becomes a "somebody". So they made birth the dividing line.

I: Why? Look at your words: "*They made* birth the dividing line." Don't you see how arbitrary it is? It's man-made, it's conventional, it's your will, your will-to-power. It's made, not found; created, not discovered. You can't give any reason for it in the nature of things. It's not based on objective truth, but on subjective desire.

L: That's not true.

I: Why? What objective fact can it be based on?

L: The simple fact that before you are born you are not a separate person, you are part of your mother. That's why birth is the reasonable dividing line.

Pro-choice argument no. 9: Fetuses are parts of persons

I: So a fetus is a part of the mother.

L: Yes.

I: So its cells are her cells, as my toe's toenails are my toenails.

L: Yes.

I: Then if the baby is a boy, his penis is his mother's penis.

L: That's ridiculous.

I: My point exactly. In fact, it's even more ridiculous than that. If fetuses are parts of mothers, then all pregnant women have eight limbs: four arms and four legs. Eight limbs! You said I confuse fetuses with persons?—I say you confuse mothers with spiders!

L: And I still say birth is a reasonable dividing line. It's how we date ourselves. We don't celebrate our first birthday three months after we're born, but twelve.

I: Of course not: three months after birth is the anniversary of our conception, not our birth.

L: Well, why don't we celebrate conception days, then, instead of birthdays?

I: Maybe because we didn't know much about conception until relatively recently, with modem science. Actually, I think the ancient Chinese did have that custom, calculating age from conception instead of birth. But you can't argue from either custom because you can't argue from customs to realities. The human race has had some terribly strange and foolish customs, you know.

Pro-choice argument no. 10: We celebrate birthdays, not conception days

L: Celebrating birthdays is not a strange and foolish custom. It's a natural wisdom, like a natural language. Because birth is a great event—but I suppose you wouldn't know about that.

I: Because I'm a man, or because I'm a fool?

L: Is that an either-or?

I: I agree that birth is a great event. But that doesn't mean conception isn't greater. Look, let's be fair. I'll give you a reason for thinking conception is more important, and you give me a reason for thinking birth is more important. My reason is this: Birth does not change what you are, only where you are and how you take oxygen.

Pro-choice
argument
no. 11:
Birth is the
beginning of
independence

L: It changes your relationship with your mother from dependence to independence.

I: No, it doesn't. An infant is still dependent on her mother after birth.

L: Sure, but she *begins* to be a little independent then—only at birth—and that independence gradually grows, throughout her life.

I: No, it begins before birth. Because viability begins before birth. Even if your mother died at eight months, you could still be delivered and survive. So dependence and independence are matters of degree, not a sudden, sharp dividing line.

L: Yes, but even so, birth is not just a matter of degree. It radically changes your relationship with your mother.

I: It does. But look at what you've just admitted, look what comes out in our natural language. You said "Birth changes your relationship with your mother." But how can I change my relationship with my mother unless she's my mother before as well as after the change? And how can she be my mother before birth unless I'm there before birth? Does she become *my* mother only when the doctor cuts the umbilical cord? Is a person created by a pair of scissors?

L: That's just a rhetorical trick. That's arguing from language.

I: Then let's argue from reality.

L: You mean *your* reality.

I: Oh, no, don't tell me you really believe that New Age nonsense! Who do you think you are, God, to create your own reality? Do you really have to fall back on nonsense metaphysics to justify abortion?

Pro-choice
argument
no. 12: No
essences

L: No, I use no metaphysics at all. You're the one who does metaphysics. You assume everything has an unchangeable essence, and you insist on defining these so-called essences—that's really your agenda in this whole argument about what the fetus is.

I: Of course it is! That's what the words mean.

L: What words?

I: "*What* the fetus *is*." "What" means essence, and "is" means being, or reality.

L: So you're really doing medieval philosophy, like a religious mystic.

I: Thinking about what things are didn't start or end with the Middle Ages. We all use the words, and we all know what they mean. There's nothing medieval, or mystical, or even religious, about them.

L: Well, I'm skeptical of your claim to know the essences of things. Especially fetuses. I don't think we know "what the fetus is".

I: We went over that one before too: If you don't know what it is, don't kill it!

L: Do you think birth control is morally wrong, too, then?

I: That depends on what kind. "Natural family planning", of course not. Abortifacients like the IUD or the "morning-after pill", yes, because that's abortion.

L: What about contraception? "The pill" or spermicidal jelly? Contraception kills potential persons, too: sperm and eggs. If you call abortion murder, then you have to call contraception murder too, because it kills potential persons. There's metaphysics for you: abortion kills only potential persons, not actual persons. The fetus is biologically human, but it's not an actual person yet, only a potential person. It may be tragic to kill a potential person; it may even sometimes be wrong, but it's not murder. Unless you say contraception is murder, too.

I: Ah, yes, the "potential person" argument. I've heard that one before. What I haven't heard is any answer to this simple question: If a fetus is only a potential person and not an actual person, what is it actually? An ape?

L: It's potential, it's not actual.

I: But to be a potential x, it has to be an actual y. To be a potential runner, I have to be an actual animal with legs. To be a potential sinner, I have to be an actual person with a free will. So what is a fetus actually? Is it an ape? A fish? A worm?

L: It's actually human but not actually personal yet. It's a potential person.

I: How can there be a potential person? I think you're confusing "a potential person" with "a person with potential", potential to function in a certain way. You're confusing the essence and the function. But the essence can't be potential. It can only be actual. It's the accidents and the actions of the thing that can be potential. For instance, an actual ape is potentially fat, or potentially swimming. But nothing is a potential ape. And nothing is a potential person.

L: This is getting more and more metaphysical and more and more confusing. And that's the main reason I'm not convinced; the failure of our argument is my main argument. There's just no way we can get everyone to agree about abortion. Different people have very different convictions about it, all deeply felt. And in a free, pluralist country like America we don't use the law to enforce a conviction that only a minority believe upon a majority who don't. There's no consensus on abortion, and the law should express consensus. That's why I'm pro-choice. I'm not pro-abortion, I'm pro-choice. You want to take away that choice and force your opinion on everybody.

Pro-choice argument no. 14: The impossibility of resolving the dispute

I: No, I don't.

L: You don't? I thought you wanted to reverse *Roe v Wade* and recriminalize abortion.

I: I do. But I want people to believe it, not just have it forced on them. You see, I'm pro-choice, too, like Moses. He said, "Choose life!" I'm both pro-choice and pro-life: I choose life, and I want everybody to do the right thing and choose life. I don't like to lose either freedom or life; I don't like either slavery or murder. And you . . . ?

L: I want to "live and let live". I don't want to force my opinions on anybody.

I: Oh, I wouldn't worry about that. That can't be done. Ever. No one can force an opinion on anybody else.

L: What? Why do you say that?

I: Because no one can take away your essence . . .

L: So?

I: . . . which includes your mind and your free will. No one can control your soul, only your body.

L: OK, but you want to control our bodies and force us to bear children. We find that the equivalent of rape. Forced motherhood. That's what you pro-lifers want to force on us.

I: Rape? That's ridiculous! If you were raped, it was the rapist who forced you to be a mother. And if you got pregnant freely, then it was not forced at all, but your choice. All we want to force you to do is not to murder your own children. Is that so unreasonable?

L: I am just about out of patience. For the last hour or so I have been getting more and more stressed and distressed by your insensitive words. You don't speak to my feelings or my experience or my identity, only my words and arguments. You know, this dialogue has been doubly one-sided: You haven't heard our side, and neither of us has talked about our feelings, our experiences. We've argued.

I: I thought I felt a lot of very strong feelings coming from you, loud and clear. I haven't stopped you from expressing any feeling at all. Have I censored you or not allowed you to emote?

L: I thought we were going to try to be non-judgmental and non-argumentative.

I: You mean you wanted to censor me and not allow me to argue, even though I allow you to emote.

L: That's a clever little argument, but in real life outside the argument it's you who want to censor us.

I: How?

L: You want to control our lives: you want to criminalize abortion.

I: We didn't criminalize it; nature did. You decriminalized it with *Roe v Wade*.

L: Which you want to reverse! You want to turn back the clock and go back to the Dark Ages.

Pro-choice argument no. 15: Historical progressivism

I: Yes, we do. We want to go back to the days when it was still a crime to kill babies, yes. We think that was the Enlightenment. We think *this* is the Dark Ages. We think *you* turned back the clock when you allowed healers to kill, to tear innocent little baby bodies into bloody bits of bone and flesh with knives and suction tubes—yes, we want to stop that.

L: Well, at least your real feelings are coming out now. I feel the heat. And I think I also understand why some of you take the law into your own hands and shoot the doctors who perform abortions. I guess that's why so many of

The parallel with gun control

you pro-lifers love the National Rifle Association and hate gun control laws.

I: Actually, the parallel with gun control works the opposite way. We want gun control in abortion clinics. We want to take the abortionist's lethal weapons away.

L: That's not a fair analogy.

I: Let's see whether it is or not. How many abortionists get shot in America each year? One or two, if that many. And how many babies get aborted? About a million and a half, I think. You're right; that's hardly a fair analogy.

L: I knew this would happen.

I: What?

L: That you'd turn nasty.

I: Oh. Killing babies isn't nasty, but talking about it is?

L: The way you talk about it, yes.

I: Without euphemism, you mean.

L: Without qualifications. Without looking at all the modifying factors and feelings and circumstances. You've talked only about one thing: the fetus (which you keep calling a baby).

I: And I've told you why.

L: And I've told you why that bugs me.

I: Tell me again.

L: You're a black-and-white thinker.

I: What do you mean by that?

L: Most of life is gray, not black or white. You impose your black-or-white cookie cutter on gray matter.

I: I refuse to take that bait. That's too easy.

L: What bait?

I: The invitation to insult your gray matter.

L: How clever of you to insult me by refusing to insult me!

I: You know, you're right. We've degenerated into insults. Both of us.

L: I told you that would happen.

I: Can we try just one more time to get to the root of the matter? I really want to know what most basically divides us, why we're so very, very different when it comes to abortion that we can't talk about it without degenerating into insult, even when we try.

L: You know, I'd like to find that out, too. OK, let's stick our heads out one more time. But let's warm up the coffee and take one more break first.

L: So here we are: third try. Do you think you could stop arguing about fetuses long enough to listen to my feelings?

I: Do you really think that's what separates us most fundamentally: feelings?

L: Don't you?

I: No.

L: Why?

I: Because feelings come and go, like breezes or measles. It shouldn't be so hard to sit light on your feelings, to understand and accept the fact that other people simply feel differently. We don't have fights about whether you love or hate yogurt.

L: So what do you think divides us? Deep-seated personality types?

I: No, arguments. Arguments that go back to different premises, different fundamental convictions. That's why I think it's more helpful to look at each other's arguments than to look at each other's feelings. We want to understand each other and where we're each coming from; and that means tracing each other's arguments back to their fundamental premises. That's what you began by doing, I think, and I should have kept on that trail. You began by voicing your annoyance, not so much at my pro-life conclusions, as at my assumption that I could be certain about them.

L: Yes. But I don't want to get into a philosophical argument about theory of knowledge and skepticism and certainty. It's too abstract.

I: Too abstract for what?

L: For my interest. And the interest of our readers. We're in a book, remember.

I: Good grief, I had forgotten that! So what do you suggest we do?

L: Examine where *I'm* coming from for a change.

I: Good. I'd really like to know that.

L: Thank you. Well, then, here are some of my deepest convictions—

I: Premises, you mean. Reasons. Convictions that entail your pro-choice conclusions.

L: Oh.

I: That is what we're dialoguing about, after all: abortion. Not you or me. Our readers don't care about *you*. You thought you weren't even real, remember? But abortion is.

L: Hmph. Well, I found your fundamental premise: your dogmatism. So I guess mine is skepticism.

Skepticism vs. Dogmatism

I: Skepticism versus dogmatism about what?

L: About the fetus. That it's a person.

I: I thought I gave quite a few reasons for believing that, and I thought I answered all your arguments against believing that. How is that dogmatism? Did I assert it dog-matically? Did I say, "Believe it not for any good reason, but because I say so"?

L: No. But don't you think our deepest difference is there? I mean, you do claim to have certain knowledge, absolute and unchangeable, but I don't.

I: No, I don't think our deepest difference is there. Be-cause I think you're more dogmatic than I am when you go by your own feeling or will instead of reasoning. And I think I'm more skeptical than you are when I say, "don't kill it if you're not sure whether it's a person", while you say it's OK to kill it. Because that's acting as if you did know.

L: Where do *you* think our deepest difference lies?

I: I don't know. Maybe in defining a person. You say the fetus isn't a person because it's not doing any of the things only persons can do, like thinking and choosing—right?

L: Right.

"Function-alism"   **I:** Well, maybe that's our deepest difference. I'd call that premise Functionalism: defining a person by her functions.

L: I notice you've started using the generic "her" instead of "his".

I: That's because this is a "feminist" point, and I'm sur-prised you missed it.

L: What do you mean, "feminist" point?

I: Women usually get this point much more easily than men: that a person is more than her functions. The first question men usually ask about somebody is: "What does he *do*?" They identify a person with his career, his function. Women are more likely to wonder about who he *is*, what kind of person he is: his being, not just his doing. That's why I think you've sold out to male chauvinism.

L: *Moi*? That's outrageous!

I: But isn't it true? Isn't it men who tend to identify themselves with what they do?

L: Yes—and why do you think that is?

I: Maybe we have to do that to get an identity, because we don't have wombs. Wombs are built-in meanings and purposes, built-in careers. We don't have them, so we have to go out and forge an identity and a career and a purpose by working at something. We have to *do* something; women just have to *be*.

L: Are you saying that makes men inferior?

I: No, just different. But I find it ironic that I would be defending the feminine concept of a person, and you would be defending the masculine concept of a person by identifying a person with her functions.

L: Her functions as distinct from what?

I: Her nature. A woman should be more sensitive to nature, and her own nature, and the nature of things, and the nature of a person.

L: Says who? That's an interesting old stereotype, but it's pure speculation. I thought you were going to give me logic instead of this vague talk about "the nature of things".

*Logic &
nature*

I: And that's another typically male gambit: demanding logic and ignoring nature. But I'll be glad to oblige if it's logic you want.

L: Oh, I'm sure you will.

I: Because I don't think there's any contradiction between being logical and being natural, or commonsensical. Common sense distinguishes between being and function, or nature and function, or what you are and what you do—and between *being* a person and *functioning* as a person. You can't function as a person without first being a person. But you can be a person without functioning as a person.

L: This is getting pretty abstract.

I: Then let me make it very concrete. When you're in deep, dreamless sleep, or in a coma, or in very early infancy, you're not thinking or choosing or doing any of those things—however you want to expand the list—that you would call the properly personal functions. Yet there's a person there. How do you know that? You can't tell just by looking at how it's functioning. It's not thinking or choosing or anything else on your list. And yet we all know there's something there, something else there besides the actions.

L: It's potentially there.

I: No, it's actually there, it's just not actually functioning. When you're sleeping, you're there, and you're a person. You don't stop being a person every time you stop consciously thinking or choosing. And we all know that. That's why we do brain surgery on a brain-damaged child but not on a chimpanzee: because we recognize that there's something there in that human infant that's not there in the chimp, something whose functioning has been retarded. If we fix the damage, the child will think and choose. But nothing we can do can make an ape think and choose.

Can we see souls?

L: So what is that "something there"?

I: Most people call it the soul.

L: But you can't see a soul. You can only see bodily acts.

I: You see a soul revealing itself in and through bodily acts. When I smile, you see my soul, or the happiness in my soul.

L: That's just a physical expression of it, a physical sign or symbol of the mental state.

I: No it's not. It's not like a word on a piece of paper, like the word "happiness". There's no happiness in the word "happiness", but there's happiness *in* a smile.

L: So how does this impact abortion?

I: The fetus has a soul. It's not yet revealing itself by performing any of the functions a chimp can't perform. But it will. The specifically human functions will come; and when they do, we will all see through them, so to speak, see the soul through them.

L: That sounds like a pretty mystical basis for outlawing abortion!

I: Not at all. It's utterly commonsensical. It's based on the distinction you don't make, the distinction between being and functioning. What could be more commonsensical than this?—you can act or function in a specially human way only because you have the specially human being, human nature. And you have human nature from the beginning. You don't change from an ape to a human in your being, only in your functioning. You confuse personal being with personal functioning. That's what I mean by "functionalism". Maybe that's our fundamental difference: on what a human person is.

L: Or maybe the difference is that I'm being scientific instead of religious. Science doesn't talk about the soul. Once you start arguing on the basis of souls, or invisible essences or "natures", you've gone beyond science.

Science, religion and common sense

I: Of course. We all do that.

L: But once you do that, you can go anywhere. You can't be refuted. A scientific theory is one that can be verified or falsified scientifically, empirically. It's like a car on a road with curbs. Religion and philosophy are like a plane in the sky: you can't bump into anything, you can't be refuted, you don't have hard data. That's why I'm skeptical about talk about "the nature of things".

I: You wouldn't talk about "the nature of a river", for instance?

L: No. The Mississippi River or the Nile or the Amazon, maybe. But all rivers are different. There's no such thing as "the nature of a river", there're just individual rivers: the Mississippi, the Nile, the Amazon. All rivers are different.

I: If all rivers are different how can you even call them all "rivers"? Don't you see? You can't even use ordinary language without contradicting yourself. The very word "all" should be struck from your vocabulary. You're a Nominalist: you reduce all universals to mere words.

Nominalism

L: I'm only being what you claim to be and aren't: simple and commonsensical. You're the one who keeps talking in that mystical, muddled, outdated, prescientific way about the essences of things, or the nature of things.

I: So talking about what a thing is is mystical and muddled and unscientific? But it's built into the structure of every language, unless you omit all common nouns. In fact, almost all words are universals.

L: What do you mean, "universals"?

I: What can be a predicate for many subjects, what can be predicated of many different individuals. For instance, "red", "man", "in", "clumsily"—they're all universals. You can't dispense with universals, or essences, or essential natures, not without dispensing with human understanding itself and lowering yourself to the animal level, the level of brute empirical fact and nothing more.

L: Thanks for the language lesson. It follows, of course, that abortion should be criminalized.

I: It follows that arguing about the essence of a thing, including a fetus, is no more mystical than children are.

L: Fine. Childish, then. But certainly not scientific.

I: Wrong again. Science seeks universals, too. What is every scientific formula but a universal?

L: Fine, so there are universals, even universal essences, if you like. But still, we know a thing's essence only by observing its functions.

I: So we know who Abraham Lincoln is only by his functional title "President of the United States"? And another man is only "the ticket puncher on the train"? You are what you do? Nothing more?

L: No, that's obviously inhuman and impersonal.

I: Why? Isn't it because we should value persons not for what they can do, what function they perform, but for what they are, for their intrinsic being? Don't you agree that we should treat all persons as ends rather than using them as means because that's the uniqueness of a person?

The intrinsic value of persons

L: I agree with that.

I: And the place where you're valued for what you are, not for what you do, is your family. It's the workplace where you're valued only for what you do, for your functioning. I think it was Robert Frost who defined "home" as "the place where, when you go there, they have to take you in".

L: I agree with that, too.

I: Then you agree with a lot of the concerns of pro-lifers about the family and love and personalism . . .

L: Certainly. Do you think we're monsters or something?

I: No, but I think you're not helping families by replacing the old "sanctity of life ethic" with the new "quality of life ethic".

'Sanctity of life' vs. 'quality of life'

L: I think we are. We want to increase the quality of life for families just as much as for individuals. It's simply unfair polemics to call that Functionalism.

I: I don't think so. When you talk about the "quality of life", you mean something we judge, right? And you judge that a human life has more value if it functions at a certain level—something from your list of personal functions, whether I.Q. or the ability to communicate and relate to other people, or freedom of will, or freedom from coercion or even freedom from paralysis—as in that Paul Newman propaganda film for euthanasia, *Whose Life Is It, Anyway*? That's why I call the "quality of life ethic" Functionalism.

L: And why do you find it so terribly wicked to be as compassionate to people as we are to our pets?

I: I find it terribly *dangerous*. If you say a life is worth living if it has an I.Q. of 50 today, what's to stop you from saying it has to have an I.Q. of 100 tomorrow, or even 150, in order to have a right to life? What's to stop Brave New World, or George Bernard Shaw's utopian society of the future, where every citizen has to appear before a central planning committee each year to justify the social utility of his existence or else be "terminated"? Painlessly, of course. That's all the "quality of life" defenders seem to care about: not the right to life but the right to a pain-free life, the right to pleasure.

L: Here we go again, into personal insult.

I: No; *philosophical* insult. I do mean to insult your philosophy. Because I think it insults me, and you, and every other person. I think it's destructive to human dignity, because it judges persons by what they can do; it reduces being to functioning. And therefore it's elitist.

L: Why do you call it elitist?

I: Because we're not equal in I.Q. or communication skills or any of those other functions; we're equal only in our essence, our essential humanity, our human nature. So if you discount the notion of "the nature of things", you have no basis for equality. And then what happens? Then it becomes naked power, "might makes right."

L: That's ridiculous.

Why don't fetuses kill doctors?

I: Is it? Not if you dare to ask one very simple question: Why do doctors kill fetuses instead of fetuses killing doctors? Fetuses don't want to be killed. They struggle to live. Did you ever see *The Silent Scream*? No, of course not; I forgot: we're not living in a free country, our media will never ever let you see that. Well, the answer to this simple little question is power. Doctors kill fetuses because doctors have power. They have the weapons, and the know-how to use them; fetuses are totally defenseless. If fetuses came equipped with little scalpels and little poison packs and could defend themselves against their killers, how many doctors do you think would perform abortions? So what makes the difference between life and death? Power. Camouflaged under the name of "healer" and dressed up in white robes and hypocritical oaths.

L: Wow! At least you're being honest and confessing your true feelings and fears. I suppose you think of us as the next thing to Mafia hit men, right?

Abortionists vs. hitmen

I: Actually, I think I would be more comfortable having dinner with a Mafia hit man than with an abortionist, because an abortionist is a paid hit man, too, a hired killer, but one who pretends he isn't.

L: Obviously, there is nothing more to say. We've passed beyond even arguable insult. Surprisingly, I'm grateful for your outburst: thank you for showing me your true feelings. And now I'll tell you mine. I'm as afraid of you as you are of me. I'm afraid of anyone who acts propelled by fears like that. I'm propelled by love; you're propelled by fear. That's our deepest difference, I think. I think I understand us now.

Love vs.
fear

I: You *don't* understand. My fears are *based on* love. If I didn't love human beings very much, I guess I wouldn't fear killing them very much, either. And if I were skeptical, like you, and I claimed no one could know whether fetuses are persons or not, I certainly would fear killing them, and I would be be pro-life—if I loved persons. But I'd have much less fear of killing persons if I *didn't* love them very much, I think that's the deepest difference between us: the value of the human person. It's not just about babies, or skepticism, or nominalism, or the role of the law, or feminism, or whether there are moral absolutes, or whether there is a God, but whether a person is so valuable that you won't even take a *chance* of killing one.

Do we give
up?

L: I refuse to accept that picture. I guess we just have to agree to disagree, and understand that there can't really be an open dialogue.

I: No we don't. We can be *bothered* that we differ—if we love the truth. And if we believe in truth, how can we give up dialoguing, no matter how hard it is?

L: *We* can give up whenever our author stops writing.

I: But our readers can't, until they stop thinking.